Unblind Faith

Unblind Faith

Michael J. Langford

SCM PRESS LTD

334 01713 0

First published 1982
by SCM Press Ltd
58 Bloomsbury Street, London WC1

Typeset by Gloucester Typesetting Services
and printed in Great Britain by
Richard Clay Ltd (The Chaucer Press),
Bungay, Suffolk

Contents

Preface

Adults who are preparing for confirmation or for church membership urgently need an introduction to the Christian faith that appeals to the head as well as to the heart. Although there can be no question of proving the truth of Christianity by purely rational methods, the faith can be, and should be, presented in a way that is attractive to the thinking person. This book is an attempt to meet the need for this kind of presentation of the Christian faith. Its primary purpose is to serve as an aid during preparation for adult confirmation. However, it can also be used as a refresher course or post-confirmation course by those already confirmed, or as a general introduction to the Christian faith for anyone who is looking for a basic statement of the faith that stresses the role of understanding.

Although this book is based on a series of talks given in an Anglican church (St Augustine's, in the city of St John's, Newfoundland), there is nothing in it which is specifically Anglican except perhaps for some of the emphases. Therefore, it may be helpful to members of other denominations who are looking for an introduction to Christianity. There are certain passages that may cause disagreement, especially on the nature of the church and on the authority of the Bible, but these may always be used as opportunities for discussion, even when there are objections to my point of view.

When this book is used as an aid to confirmation preparation, I would like to stress that it does not attempt to teach everything that a candidate should know. For example, he or she will certainly need instruction in prayer and public worship, and in practical Christian ethics, which things this book does not attempt to give. However, the candidate may find here a useful survey of the fundamentals of Christian teaching and of a Christian philosophy of life, both of which are essential elements in preparation for adult church membership.

I also hope that this book will be read by some non-Christians who want an introduction to the Christian faith with a rational emphasis. For such readers I would indicate that, except for chapter XIV, the main purpose of this book is not that of showing that the Christian faith is true, but that of showing what it is.

Finally, I should like to point out that I have frequently used 'he' instead of 'he or she' throughout this book. This is purely a matter of style. In almost all cases I mean the generic 'he', equivalent to 'he or she'.

PART ONE

THE ESSENTIALS OF THE CHRISTIAN FAITH

I Faith and Reason

Blind faith

The truth is often discovered to be a middle ground between two extremes, both of which are false and dangerous. One must not make a dogma out of this, as if the truth were necessarily the middle position, for sometimes an extreme position may turn out to be true. However, there is much to be said for an initial sympathy with the middle way and, with this as a starting point, I shall argue in this chapter that Christian faith should be seen as a kind of middle way between 'blind faith' on the one hand and a 'purely rational faith' on the other.

Let us look first at blind faith. By this I mean an absolute, unconditional, and unexamined trust in God, or in some person who is believed to represent him, or in some body of teaching about God. Usually this blind faith goes hand in hand with absolute obedience to what is believed to be the will of God, as interpreted by a book or a prophet. This is to describe blind faith in its religious form, but it has also a secular counterpart such as absolute, unconditional and unexamined trust in a political party, or a leader, or a set of duties set down by custom or by the state.

It needs little reflection to show that this kind of unconditional trust is a mistake and, indeed, part of the very nature of blind faith consists precisely in the denial of the right to start such reflection, for the very idea of reflection on a belief or practice suggests that some kind of justification should be sought for it.

One way of indicating the mistaken nature of blind faith is to look at some of its recent results. We can recall the fanatical followers of

Jim Jones who not only took cyanide themselves but fed it to their children at Jones-town in Guyana; also the fanatical mobs which shout for the Ayatollah Khomeini, or for some other religious leader, and which seem to be incapable of rational reflection; also the daily brain-washing of new converts in many of the fringe sects; and so on. Unfortunately the history of Christianity and of many other religions is sprinkled with the dire consequences of blind faith and it is the horror of this spectacle that helps in large measure to explain the rejection of all religion by many thoughtful people. While I believe that this total rejection is a mistake, it is perfectly understandable, for when religion is judged by such examples, the genuinely good man is under a moral obligation to reject it.

A second, and deeper, ground for rejecting blind faith comes from the following reflection, a reflection that has probably already occurred to many readers in a similar form. Here I am, let us say an adult Christian. What would I be if I had been brought up as a Buddhist in Burma, or as an atheistic Marxist in Russia? I would probably be a Buddhist or a Marxist. Does this prove that people simply believe what they have been told and that reason has nothing to do with belief? No, this is too severe, because some people do abandon or change their childhood beliefs and so others must be capable of acts of reflection which have led them to confirm their early beliefs, though usually with certain modifications. But the very existence of the great variety of possible beliefs must force us to ask ourselves, why this one rather than that one? If blind faith were acceptable, then it would be proper for one to have blind faith in Christianity and another in Marxism and so on. But such a suggestion is absurd, for even if it is the case that the great religions have a common core, there are many faiths that disagree profoundly with others and they could not all be right. There is only one rational response to this situation and that is that blind faith is never justified.

Reflection such as the above leads me to suspect that blind faith is not only a mistake, but is essentially demonic or evil. If one happens to be following a good master with a blind faith, this is only by chance and there is a despotic element in the relationship which the good master does not want and which prevents personal growth. Much more likely is blind faith in a master who likes this kind of devotion and then both the relationships and the actual commands will probably end up as evil.

At this point, the reader who is sensitive to the Christian tradition might well say, 'Hold it. Surely there is something noble and beautiful about absolute and unconditional faith, despite these negative examples. What about Jesus' call to single-mindedness,[1] and what about that complete faith that sustains Christians when they are faced with persecution, or apparently impossible burdens, or death?' But a crucial distinction must be made here. Absolute faith that something is true, or that someone is to be obeyed, is one thing. This is the blind faith that asks for no reason, but which simply sees the faith as its own justification. Quite another thing is a faith that has been grounded in something other than the faith itself, in other words a faith which one has some kind of reason for holding and which one then holds to in the face of enormous pressure.

The misunderstanding here arises because the idea of an 'unconditional' faith is ambiguous. When the unconditional element refers to the acceptance of something as true or someone as an absolute leader, then there is a dangerous irrationality. When the unconditional element refers to the way in which one 'sticks to one's guns' in a time of trial, this is not a case of irrationality but of courage. In the former case, one is resisting the onslaught of reason; in the latter, the onslaught of weariness or pain or temptation. The former is blind faith, the latter is heroic faith.

A purely rational faith?

Let us look next at the religious position which is at the opposite extreme to blind faith, that of a purely rational faith. What I mean by this is the view that the essentials of the faith can either be proved by a rational process, or at the very least rendered as highly probable as some of our scientific beliefs. Few contemporary Christians take such an extreme position, but it is easy to find Christian views which tend in this direction. For example, according to orthodox Roman Catholicism, the existence and essential nature of God can be rigorously proved in the ways that Aquinas indicated, even though there are other truths that depend upon the acceptance of revelation. An equally strong rational tradition can be found within Anglicanism, for example among the Cambridge Platonists, though it has never had official sanction.

What should be said about this rational approach to faith? In this

3

case, my criticisms are much less severe than in the case of blind faith for I hold that there are rational grounds of a kind for Christianity, and that no doctrine should be believed without some rational support. We might recall here the advice given in the first epistle of Peter: 'Always be prepared to make a defence to any one who calls you to account for the hope that is in you . . .'[2] (Some translations speak of giving a 'reason' for the hope that is in you.) However, the claim that we can *prove* the essentials of the faith in any ordinary sense of the word, for example, in the way in which scientists seek to prove things, is a mistake.

The principal argument against seeking a strict proof in matters of faith will become clearer in the next chapter when we discuss the meaning of the word 'God'. The essential point is this. If God is a reality of the kind claimed in the Christian tradition (and also in the Jewish and Islamic traditions), then he cannot be comprehended within any system of knowledge. He is rather the one whose presence evokes awe and amazement and either silence or the sort of utterance that we find on the tongue of Isaiah or Job.[3] Whatever our personal views or our personal experiences may be, it is a fact that in all ages men and women have had these overpowering experiences which led them to believe that they were in the presence of God. These experiences are part of the foundation of the great religions of the world and, in the light of them, any attempt to comprehend or to understand God fully is absurd. It follows that a rational proof of divine reality is equally absurd, for this would involve in some way containing or understanding God within a wider system of knowledge.

Another way of putting the same point goes as follows. Reason itself can see its own limitations and that when we use the word 'proof' we use it in a certain context. For example, within natural science we may properly say that we have proved certain things (though not with the same kind of certainty that applies to mathematical proofs), when we have carried out certain procedures. For example, we can say that we have proved that water contains hydrogen and oxygen as a result of the systematic tests that have been carried out. But in this kind of procedure we are always explaining one part of the universe by its relation to other parts. However, when we try to explain the universe *as a whole*, or when, even more puzzlingly, we talk about a being who is not part of the universe at all, then the procedures that are appropriate to natural science are inappropriate. It does not follow in the least that questions about God are absurd or irrational, but it does follow that they are not scientific questions, and that the very notion of proof as we normally use it (in science, mathematics or law) is inapplicable.

Unblind faith

So far I have argued against two extreme positions; blind faith, which I hold to be irrational, dangerous and even demonic, and a purely rational faith, which I hold to be impossible given the kind of reality that Christians claim God to be. I want next to explain further what I mean by the middle way, the way which I propose to call 'unblind faith', and to argue that it constitutes the only acceptable approach to belief by the thoughtful Christian.

In the first place, we must remember that we are thinking about faith, not simply belief, and a realization of what this involves can help us to see that a purely rational faith is not only a mistake, but an impossibility. Whereas many of our *beliefs* do not affect us in our way of life (for example, most of our beliefs about the past, or about scientific claims which we think to be true but which we have not yet been able to prove), *faith* always affects our way of life. With faith, in addition to belief that something is the case, there is a commitment that some people describe as an *existential* commitment because of the way in which it affects the very way in which we exist as persons. For example, the loyal worker for a political party does not only believe that his party's programme is true in some abstract way, he has faith in it. Similarly, people do not only believe in the virtues of their close friends, they have faith in them; similarly too, Christians not only believe that God is a reality, they have faith in him. The point is sometimes expressed in this way: Christians do not only believe *that* God is real, they believe *in* God, for faith is a belief *in* something or someone. It follows again that this cannot be a purely rational matter because not only the mind but also the heart and will are involved.

In the second place, since we are considering an unblind faith, there must be grounds for it of some kind that appeal to our reason. These grounds cannot amount to proof, for the reasons that I have given, and they must be appropriate to the kind of reality with which we are concerned, namely God. What these grounds are will become clearer as

5

this book proceeds, but we have a clue in the words of St Paul when he describes how one day we shall *know*, but for now we must be content with puzzling reflections in a mirror.[4] That is to say, we must build as best we can on the intimations and glimpses of a higher reality that we are able to have.

Faith and doubt

We must now face an extremely important question that touches a large number of people. There are many who search for a faith, but who experience grave doubts not only about secondary matters but about the very existence of God. The question then arises, can one have faith in God while experiencing such doubts? Christians have answered this question in different ways, but my own convictions are as follows. In the short run the answer is certainly yes. We are never asked to smother our intellectual curiosity and therefore, almost inevitably, Christians will have periods of doubt or uncertainty, but if they continue to try to lead the Christian life and generally to live through this period *as if* they were convinced of the reality of God, then this is a continuation of the life of faith. This involves no dishonesty, unless one claims a certainty that one does not possess. Once again, an example from a non-religious faith can illuminate the matter. If I promise to follow the leader of an expedition into the unknown and to trust him when there is a crisis, I am not promising never to have doubts. I am promising to follow in spite of any doubts that may arise along the way. Similarly, the thoughtful Christian knows that he is likely to have periods of doubt in which acts of will and determination will have to carry him through.

But what if the doubts persist for weeks or months; can there still be a viable Christian faith? There can be no simple answer here for each person's own story is different. Undoubtedly, there can come a point where honesty should compel the searcher to say, 'I am no longer a Christian, I am an agnostic', but there are many kinds of persistent doubt where this step is not called for. Let us suppose, by way of example, that a certain Christian has a long period of doubt about the reality of God, but that he remains convinced that there is a real possibility that God exists, so that, from an intellectual point of view, Christianity is what has been called a 'living option'.[5] Also, he remains attracted to the Christian way of life, finding himself drawn to it on account of its moral appeal and the sense which it begins to make of his world. In the light of all this, he decides to live in accordance with the Christian model as he sees it, so he attempts both to live and to pray in the way that Jesus taught. In my judgment, such a man can call himself a Christian and he can continue to affirm the first Christian creed, 'Jesus is Lord',[6] with complete honesty. I suspect that this example is far more typical of the Christian man or woman than is generally realized and it is important to see it as a legitimate variation on the theme of Christian faith.

Unblind faith and the New Testament

In order to strengthen our grasp of the meaning of unblind faith, I want next to show how the description of faith that I have given accords with the way in which faith is represented in the New Testament.

If there were a person to whom blind obedience should be given, then surely this would be to God or, for the Christian, to his only son Jesus Christ. However, the philosophy of God and of man that I shall outline in the next chapters suggests that the last thing that God wants is a blind obedience, even to himself, for this would be a denial of the *human* response that he wants to draw from us. It is utterly congruous with this suggestion to see that Jesus, while calling people to follow him, avoided giving his teaching in the form of absolute truths, but rather used suggestive stories and poetic phrases. Also, when asked a direct question, he nearly always asked a question in return. As with Socrates, he seems to have felt that if we would know a truth, that is really know it is as opposed merely to being able to give a correct answer which we could not go on to explain, then we must discover it for ourselves. The true teacher can sometimes help to draw this truth out from us, but he cannot simply give it to us.

With this in mind, let us return to the example of the doubt-filled Christian given in the last section, but place him in the time of Jesus' earthly ministry. He is attracted to all that Jesus stands for and wants to follow him. He is happy to call him 'Lord' despite his doubts about the reality of God, for he wishes to risk being his disciple and to enthrone in his own life the values that Jesus teaches. Let us suppose that after the death of Jesus, although not one of the five hundred who claimed to have seen the risen Jesus,[7] he continues as a disciple, being baptized as he pronounces the first creed, and that he subsequently

7

dies a martyr's death for the faith. Most of us would describe this as a triumphant Christian life because the most important element in faith is the faithfulness that is shown in the way we live and to the person we follow. Beliefs *about* the nature of God or the status of Jesus are secondary. But if this is the root of faith in the New Testament, doubts in themselves need not prevent us from being and from calling ourselves Christians.

This understanding of the nature of faith should explain the use of the term 'Christian agnostic', which is puzzling to many people, but which has been used by a number of deeply committed Christians in order to describe their point of view.[8] Strictly speaking, the word 'agnostic' simply means 'one who does not know' and since Christians claim to believe, rather than to know, there is no reason why a Christian cannot be 'agnostic' about the reality of God. In popular usage, of course, the word refers to someone who neither knows nor believes and, in order not to cause confusion, I shall normally use the word in this sense. However, the use of the term 'Christian agnostic' does serve a useful purpose. It reminds us, first, that Christians do not claim *knowledge* of God in this life; second, that doubt is not the opposite of faith. The opposite of faith is faithlessness.

Hebrew and Greek

Within the early church, some disciples had a Hebrew background and some a Greek background. This is important because it indicates the *comprehensiveness* of the church, both in its first years and in our own time. Christians are united in their love and devotion to Jesus, but they do not all have the same world view in all respects, nor the same approach to faith. Because the Hebrew and the Greek represent *types* of person that we still find, I shall outline the difference in their approaches. In doing this, I shall be forced to oversimplify the issues grossly and I shall have to lump all Hebrews and all Greeks together in a way which cannot do justice to the individuals that actually made up these races. Nevertheless, this review of the difference between typical Hebrew and typical Greek can serve two useful purposes for us. It can help us to understand how Christian philosophy developed as a response to both traditions and it can help us to appreciate the fact that the church holds within itself a great variety of people and views.

Whereas the Hebrews thought of God as the one who had delivered the Jews from Egypt and saw Christ as the long expected Messiah foretold by the great prophets, some of the Greeks started with an idea of God that was much less personal. God was the supreme principle by which all things could be explained, or the ultimate reality that lay behind the world that we could see.

Of particular influence on Christianity was the view of Plato and this was familiar to many of the first Christians who came from a Greek background. Ultimate reality, for Plato, was the Good, the True and the Beautiful, and these three were somehow united in the 'One', that supreme reality by which alone the multiplicity of our experiences can be made sense of. It followed that whoever followed or sought after what is good, or true, or beautiful, was in some sense seeking after God. Moreover, when Jesus is called the 'Word' in St John's gospel,[9] the actual word used is *logos*, which is Greek not only for 'word' but for 'reason'. This was highly suggestive and attractive to those with a Platonic education, for they could then see Jesus as the expression, or model in human form, of the perfectly good and true and beautiful.

Christian teaching about God is the result of a complex blending of the Hebrew and Greek cultures. Some Christians find this an embarrassment for Christianity and so one sometimes hears preachers calling for us to purify our faith by removing the Greek influence and returning to the strictly biblical view. I take the opposite stand and hold that the blending of Hebrew and Greek views was one of the things which enriched Christian teaching and enabled it to conquer both the hearts and the minds of all kinds of people in the ancient world, including many of the most intellectually gifted. The Christian God is the God of the Old Testament *and* the Father of Jesus *and* the supreme principle by which alone man can hope to begin to understand all things. This does not make for an easy or simple philosophy, but why should we think that the truth is easy or simple? There may indeed be a kind of 'simplicity', or singleness of vision which the truly good can reach, but very often the request to make everything simple is a cowardly request, a demand for an easy answer whether or not it is the true answer! I believe in Christianity because I believe that it is true, but the truth is something which we can reach only, if at all, by hard work. In one sense Christian faith is simple; it is that trust which enables one to say 'Jesus is Lord'. But when we are asked to say what our faith teaches us about the nature of God, or man, or Jesus, then we have no right to demand simple answers. We must follow the argument and the evidence where they lead. (When Jesus said that we should become like little children, I suggest that he was referring to the innocence and to the boundless imagination that many children have. Surely he was not asking us to smother our intellectual curiosity?)

Let us see the import of all this for the idea of an unblind faith. A blind faith might express a genuine search for what is good and beautiful, but it cannot possibly express a search for what is true. A purely rational faith might express a search for what is true, but it cannot by itself express a striving for what is good and beautiful. Thus, if we seek a faith that is adequate for our vision of God, it must be an unblind faith, of the kind that I have attempted to describe.

Finally, let us return to the problem that faces the person who is seeking God, but who feels that he has not found him and that he has no faith. Pascal said that one would not be seeking God unless one had already found him. From what has been said about God as the Good and the True and the Beautiful, we can now see why, in a sense, this must be true. Furthermore, we have the biblical promise that those who truly seek God will find him, a promise that is powerfully expressed in Mendelssohn's oratorio, *Elijah*: 'If with all your hearts ye truly seek me, ye shall ever surely find me.'[10]

II The Idea of God

What we mean by 'God'

If one is trying to understand Christianity, the first question to ask is not 'Does God exist?', but 'What do we mean by God?' All sorts of people use the word 'God' in many different religions and, although there are connections between the different uses of the word, it is by no means obvious that all people mean the same thing. Sometimes when I hear an atheist say that he does not believe in God, I find out on further inquiry that he has what seems to me such a peculiar idea of what God is that I am tempted to say that I do not believe in God either, that is *in his sense of the word*! Since there are these different ideas about God and since some people deny that the word has any meaning at all, there is no point in trying to decide whether God is a reality until we have begun to understand what we mean by the term. In this chapter, I shall try to lay the foundations for such an understanding, based on the conviction that within the tradition that is common to Judaism, Christianity and Islam the word 'God' does have a coherent meaning which, to a certain degree, can be brought out and explained.

I stress that the explanation can only be 'to a certain degree' because, when we reflect on the matter, there must seem to be a sort of absurdity in the attempt to write about the idea of God even in a long book, let alone in a short chapter. How could one define or describe God? The very attempt suggests that one is treating God as a thing within the universe rather than as its source and that one just does not understand the idea. Nevertheless, some things can be said which begin to remove some of the false conceptions of God and other things can be said which often evoke or call forth an understanding of God, even though he cannot be defined in any straightforward way.

It is important to note that many of our other fundamental concepts cannot easily be defined either. For example, consider our use of the words space, time, consciousness, freedom, life, understanding, happiness, beauty, to list but a few. We need all these words and if we abandoned them because of the fact that they cannot be defined in a straightforward way, as can words such as table, red, and mammal, then we would simply have to introduce new words to play their roles. So it appears that none of our fundamental concepts can be defined in a simple way, even though we can learn how to understand them and to use them. Therefore, the peculiar difficulty that we face in trying to deal with the word 'God' is no ground by itself for rejecting the idea of God, for such difficulties are typical of fundamental concepts.

How then can we begin to understand the idea of God? The answer I suggest is that we can start with an historical approach in which we observe the stages by which the idea has grown, especially when an old tradition has been stretched in order to make room for a new vision. Next, this historical approach must be combined with reflection on our own experience.

I am not suggesting that this is the way in which we first learned to use or understand the idea of God, for in many cases this may have happened the other way round, but that this is a good way of approaching the problem as we reflect on it now.

I have already pointed out that the Christian faith has origins in both Hebrew and Greek thought; with this in mind, let us proceed by looking at the historical development of the idea of God within these two backgrounds.

The Hebrew background

There are many ways of reading the Old Testament. If we read it as straight history, we find a fascinating story, but also a terrible one that is not at all edifying in many places and which often presents sub-Christian ideas about God. Also, we come across some passages that must strain our credulity if we have any historical sense. On the other hand, if we read the Old Testament as pure myth, although we are provided with many powerful symbols, we lose a sense of realism and vitality. A third approach and, I shall later argue, the best one, is to read it as a mixture of history and myth in which we can observe a *development* in the human understanding of God. For example, in the book of Joshua we do not learn that God wanted the Hebrews to slaughter the women and children of Jericho and Ai,[1] but that the Hebrews at that time *believed that God so willed*. Thus the history reveals not only what the Jews did, but what they believed about God. Similarly, the myths reveal how they thought about God at a certain point in time. Approached in this way, the Old Testament begins to make new sense; a drama unfolds in which we see new ideas about God emerging and we need no longer be embarrassed by the early, primitive ideas about God. This emergence can be described in terms of three stages, though this suggests a tidier scheme than the reader of the Old Testament will actually find, for the three stages constantly overlap.

During the first stage, we observe the emergence of the *one* God from the many tribal gods of the ancient world. This happens gradually for between polytheism (belief in many gods) and monotheism (belief in one God) there is usually an intermediate belief called henotheism, meaning a belief in many gods, one of whom is superior to any of the others. Gradually the superiority of this chief god is advanced until he becomes different *in kind* from the other gods and then we begin to slide over into monotheism. Examples of this intermediate belief can be found in many places in the Old Testament. One is where the Hebrew God is angry because he has been described as a god of the hills, but not a god of the plains, so that it is not wise to fight Jews in hilly country.[2] Another is where the psalmist says, 'Blessed is the nation whose God [*elohim*] is the Lord [*yahweh*]'.[3] The Hebrew word *elohim*, it should be explained, is used in some places to mean 'god' in the sense of one of the gentile gods and in others to mean the one God. In essence then the psalmist is saying our god is the Lord, your god is not.

The emergence of the idea of *one* God was of enormous importance and influence. Some think that it resulted from contact with the Egyptian monotheism of the pharaoh Ikhnaton, who probably lived at about the time of Moses; some think it the result of a personal revelation to the patriarchs; others see it as logical development as the world was increasingly seen to be *one* world, with the same laws pertaining everywhere. Perhaps it was a mixture of all three of these influences. In any case, the point is that there is progress in the idea of God, both intellectually, since a unified approach to the world becomes necessary, and morally, because all mankind is comprehended under the same creative care.

During the second stage, we observe the emergence of the idea that

God is not only powerful, but righteous. This can be seen most clearly in the development of the notion of holiness. At first, this is a reference to the danger, one might almost say contagion, likely to be suffered when one gets close to the awesome God. The purity demanded before an approach is made is a ritual purity. Shoes must be taken off on the holy mountain, various washings must take place, not for reasons of hygiene, but for ritual cleanliness. All sorts of other taboos must be observed lest one be instantly destroyed. In most cases these taboos have nothing to do with morality as we know it. For example, consider the case of Uzzah who touched the ark in order to stop it from falling and was instantly struck dead.[4] The rational approach to this passage is similar to that in which God is said to have ordered the slaughter of women and children, in that we see what people believed about God, not what God actually commanded (I will take up this point again in chapter XII). What probably happened is that poor Uzzah died of a heart attack when he realized that he had broken a taboo, but the account illustrates perfectly how people of the time thought about God's holiness.

Gradually we can watch this old notion of holiness giving way to the claim that God is righteous, in the sense of caring for how we treat our neighbour and the stranger at our gate. There is certainly a suggestion of this moral dimension to the concern of God in the second half of the Ten Commandments, which might go back to the time of Moses, but the implications of this seem hardly to have been seen until we come to the time of the great prophets, like Micah, who gave us this magnificent passage around 700 BC: 'What does the Lord require of you but to do justice, and to love kindness, and to walk humbly with your God?'[5] Other prophets of the time make explicit reference to God's concern with how we treat others, especially the poor, and Isaiah actually identifies God's holiness with this kind of righteous concern.[6]

The emergence of the third stage in this development of the idea of God makes for compelling reading, as indeed do the other stages if we are sensitive to the drama that is unfolding in the Old Testament. In this last stage, we see the stern and righteous God becoming also the loving and merciful God. We can find suggestions of this in the author of the later chapters of Isaiah and in Jeremiah, but it is most obvious in the prophet Hosea. The central theme in this prophet is the loving-kindness of God and he illustrates this by acting out a parable in front of his listeners. He marries a faithless prostitute, thereby symbolizing how God is prepared to love and care for Israel, even though she has been faithless and wanton. Here we are beginning to get close to the idea of God that enables Jesus to call him *Abba*, Father.

The Greek background

We have seen that the Hebrew background to the Christian idea of God was not one of a single and unchanging idea, but rather a story of rival views of God, with certain dominant themes emerging to produce a more or less orthodox doctrine of God by the time of Jesus. The Greek background is even more diverse: some Greeks believed in a personal God or gods, some were atheists, a small but influential minority had a philosophical notion of God as a supreme principle. Such was the importance of this last group for later thought that we must now examine its beliefs more carefully.

As we saw in the first chapter, one theme within Greek philosophy was the search for a unifying principle by which all could be explained. This search lies behind the apparently bizarre claims of some of the early philosophers, such as 'all is water' or 'all is fire'. The crucial thing here is that they were able to ask questions about everything, or the 'all', which in itself shows an advance in view parallel to the Hebrew discovery of the one God who ruled over all. One of these early philosophers suggested that 'all is mind'.[7] He did not mean that everything was made out of mind, but something closer to the idea expressed in a sentence such as this: 'Everything that there is makes some kind of sense and has an explanation that thought can grasp.' It was not very difficult to go from this to the idea that a supreme intellect, or mind, lay behind all things. This in fact became the position of some of the great philosophers and some of them called this mind *theos*, the Greek word for 'God'. But this God was not a creator, nor even a maker, who had somehow fashioned the world out of some kind of primeval matter. This act of making was left to a demigod, while God himself was left in a splendid isolation, not directly in contact with anything (for they thought that this would demean God), but drawing all things to him and enlightening all things. Plato used the material sun as an analogy for this God. The sun does not know us, but it illuminates us, and stands both for the highest and most beautiful thing that there is and for that which allows us to see. Aristotle, too, had God as the pinnacle

15

of his heavenly hierarchy, but so distant that he could not know us, though we could contemplate him. The idea of friendship with God he regarded as absurd.

Why, it may well be asked, were ideas such as these so crucial for the development of Christianity? The principle answer is this. If Christianity were to win out in the ancient world, it had to satisfy the basic longings and searchings of all men. It was not enough to provide an active personal God, or even a personal saviour. God had also to satisfy men's intellectual striving. This didn't mean that they could actually hope to comprehend God, but that he had to be the Mind behind the created order, in whom all things had an ultimate explanation and whom, in the end, we could hope both to love with our hearts and grasp with our minds. Therefore Christianity took over from the Greeks the idea that God is Mind, though they rejected the view that this mind is impersonal and cannot be known in friendship.

This many-sided human striving is as true today as in the world of the first Christians and helps to explain the complex character of the word 'spiritual'. Man's search for forgiveness, love and friendship, is part of his spiritual nature; so, too, is his questioning and searching mind. Indeed the true scientist, historian and philosopher are just as much evidence that man has a spiritual dimension as are the poet, the artist, the saint and the lover.

Anthropomorphism

Let us now move on from the historical background to the Christian idea of God to the development of the idea of God in our own individual minds. There cannot be a total change in approach here, for my individual awareness has developed in the context of a knowledge of Christianity and I am likely to interpret any private experience in the light of the religion I know. Nevertheless, there is a change of emphasis as we look at how the idea of God forms in a particular individual.

First of all, in so far as a personal God is conceived at all in childhood, he is almost certain to be conceived as a kindly old man. When children are taught to go beyond such nursery ideas and learn that God is everywhere, and perfect, and eternal, many aspects of the human model still remain. This building of God in man's image is called 'anthropomorphism' and to some degree it is inescapable for the Christian (or Jew or Muslim) if he is to talk about God at all. The very claim that God is personal, or that he is Mind, reflects our understanding of the human person and human mind. Again, words like 'love' and 'father' when applied to God get their initial meaning from human experience.

It is easy to see why many people attack Christianity, and any other religion that talks of a personal God, in the use of words such as these to describe God. All we are doing, it is alleged, is building the sort of God we would like out of our ideal picture of man.

To this attack the Christian who holds an unblind faith has a reply which it is important to be able to make and to understand. It goes like this. Certainly there is a danger here, and lots of people describe God and think of him far too much in terms of a human model, but it does not follow that we cannot use human terms such as 'father' at all, provided that we realize that we are using *analogies*. The important thing here is the Christian belief that God chose to make man in his image[8] and therefore that at his best man really can reflect something of the nature of God. Thus, when we see in a human life or in a human family the emergence of self-conscious awareness, freedom, creativity, love, and the other aspects of man that belong to him as *man*, that is as the kind of creature that God intended, then we see what was always intended to be a reflection of the creative power that made him. So in one sense anthropomorphism is bad, as it is a self-centred likening of God to a super-human; in another sense it is inevitable and, within certain limits, perfectly legitimate. What we have to remember is that what we see in man can only be an *image* of God, a puzzling reflection in a glass, though Christians believe that there is one particular image which does properly reflect the nature of God in so far as a being in space and time can do so, namely Jesus of Nazareth.

Revelation and the numinous

So far, I have indicated two of the ways in which the idea of God is built up, one historical, the other our experience of through people. However, neither of these ways by itself tells us how we can have an idea of God that is not ultimately of our own making. What needs to be added is the notion of revelation, of the claim that it is not simply a matter of man searching around in his understanding, but of God reaching down to man and in some way *showing* himself, or revealing himself to him. This is the third part of the answer to the question of how we come by an idea of God, and it lies behind the other two, for in order for them to make sense, we have to believe that God has revealed himself to men and women in the past and that he reveals himself now through men and women whom we meet.

The sceptical response to this is to ask how we know that a God has revealed himself and that it is not just a case of our unconscious mind playing tricks, or of our jumping to the wrong interpretation of some quite normal and earthly experience. The Christian reply to this is that, strictly speaking, we cannot *know* that it is God who shows himself and we cannot fully satisfy the kind of demand for proof or strong evidence that the sceptic is probably asking for, because this demand is itself loaded. It usually expects us to be able to give the sort of proof or evidence that would be appropriate for showing that a physical thing existed, not for showing that there was a spiritual source for the whole physical order. But the Christian can offer rational grounds for his belief *of an appropriate kind* and, as I have promised, I shall turn to these in chapter XIV.

If we return to the claim that God shows himself to man in certain ways, then there is one particular kind of experience that I want to stress and this is often called the sense of the *numinous*. It is impossible to describe this experience accurately, but fortunately many people have had some glimmering of it in their own lives and they will be able to recognize what I am attempting to describe. Sometimes it arises in the context of the awareness of great natural beauty, sometimes it arises quite unexpectedly for no reason that we can see, but when it comes it is an overwhelming sense of being in the presence of a being that is other than ourselves and that is at the same time awesome and fascinating. There is a sense of the uncanny and mysterious that frightens, but at the same time a sense of beauty and mystery that attracts and captivates us. Many writers have tried to describe this experience, but all admit of the near total inadequacy of our words.[9]

There is no doubt that these numinous experiences occur and that they occur to all sorts of different people in all the great religions of the world, although they are interpreted in different ways. My point is that it is this kind of experience that has helped to give force and shape to the ideas of God in all the great religions and that has helped the ordinary worshipper to understand what is meant by the divine. God is not just an abstract idea, nor even a personal being that is believed to have spoken to our forefathers, but is to some degree encountered by ordinary worshippers in the glimpses they have had of the numinous. For them, too, he is a terrifying but beautiful reality in whose presence they have been.

Of course not all people have had an experience of the numinous, even in the form of a hint or suggestion of a mysterious presence, and for them it is that much harder to give force to the idea of God. The following illustration may help to explain its power for those who do experience it. In certain psychological states, often induced by drugs, physical objects take on an incredible immediacy. People seem to be aware of their texture and colour as if for the first time, with an amazing vividness and intimacy. In a similar way, those who have really experienced the numinous tend to say that they have encountered the living presence of the divine, with an immediacy that is overpowering and that is at the same time both fearful and wonderful.

Faith and the idea of God

We have now reviewed the principal ingredients of the Christian idea of God and this is enough to show why there cannot be a simple definition of God. In traditional Christianity, God is said to be 'simple', but this is a reference to the fact that he is not made up of parts, like a physical object. 'Simple' here is contrasted with 'composite'. On the other hand, our understanding of God arises through many strands of past Christian experience and through many varieties of our own experience. There is the historical saga of the discovery of the one God who is both righteous and loving; there is the intellectual search for the Mind that orders all things; there is the experience of what is good and noble in man; there is the terrifying experience of the numinous. All of these elements are somehow brought together within the Christian idea of God, of the one who is said to be the source and ground of the physical universe, but not a part of it: a spiritual reality that has no location in space or time and yet who watches over and enters into all space and all time. Most of all, the Christian would say, a being who is the source of what is most strange and wonderful about man, his mind and his love, and these two things above all else point to the being that planned their emergence in man. So he can be called *Love*, reflecting the insight of the Hebrews, or he can be called *Mind*, reflecting the insight of the Greeks. The other two names that are most appropriate come directly from the Bible; the Old Testament name for God, 'I am who I am',[10] sometimes translated as 'he who is', and the New Testament word used by Jesus, *Abba*, the Aramaic for Father.[11]

Why has it been necessary to stress the difficulty of talking about God and to provide what some Christians may find a very academic discussion of the nature of God? Because without some grasp of the full richness of the idea of God, the mature Christian will inevitably grow out of his faith and find that his God is too small. Perhaps most of those who reject their faith, or who just let it fade away, have rejected not the Christian God, but some caricature of it that they had long since grown out of.

Some of the questions that people ask Christians or ask themselves indicate this failure to let the idea of God grow. For example, the questions 'Where is God?' and 'Who made God?' cannot be answered, not because Christianity demands a blind faith, but because the questions themselves betray a misunderstanding of the idea of God. The proper reply is to show why these questions are question-begging, because they already imply atheism. If God could be located, or if his being depended on something else, he could not correspond to the Christian idea of God.

Another example of a common question that is based on a misunderstanding of the nature of God goes, 'Why does God allow suffering?' and I shall explain this in chapter X. Yet another goes, 'Why worship this God?' When this means 'Why should we go to church or sing hymns?', this is a perfectly reasonable question to ask and I shall turn to it in chapter VII. However, the question is often much broader in scope and questions the very notion of worship, as if God could be interested in man's flattery. In this form, the question is another example of an inadequate awareness of the idea of God, for true worship is totally unlike the flattery offered to a human monarch. Worship is the word we use to express the only possible response of man to God when he begins to see him as he is. Plato thought that the physical sun was the best symbol for his God, because it was that splendid and beautiful fire that invited us to contemplate with joy the still greater beauty of God. The Christian idea of God owes much to Plato, for the Christian, too, feels drawn to gaze, not only at the sheer beauty of the things that God has made, but, if he can, at the absolute beauty of God himself. This is the true context of adoration and of worship.

III The Story of Man

What is man?

More light will be shed on the idea of God during the course of this book because the fundamental ideas that man uses come to be understood through their relationships with other ideas. Therefore, as we explore ideas such as those of man and of Christ, we shall also be adding to our understanding of the idea of God.

'What is man?' the psalmist asked[1] and in different ways just about every thinking person has asked the same question. We must note that it is not primarily a scientific question, but a value question and what philosophers would call a metaphysical question. There is, of course, a scientific question 'What is man?', which can be answered, at least in part, by modern biology and zoology. Man is an organism with certain characteristics, physiologically related to certain other organisms. I have no quarrel with such a reply to the scientific question, but it does not help us to answer the value question. When the psalmist asked 'What is man?', he was asking, in a kind of shorthand, questions such as the following: 'What is the meaning and purpose of man?', 'Where does man fit into the scheme of things?' and 'What ought man to be striving for?'

At this point, the sceptic will very likely say that these questions have no meaning and that to demand an answer is itself to beg the question of whether or not man has some kind of purpose. There is some point to this complaint, but it must be realized that the sceptic's rejection of these ancient questions is just as much the taking of a stand as the religious person's insistence that these questions must be asked. Part of what it means to have faith in God is precisely to believe that questions like 'Why does anything exist?' and 'What is the meaning of life?' are real questions which have answers, while a large part of what it means to be a sceptic is the denial that they are real questions. Thus the sceptic's complaint does not produce a new argument against a Christian philosophy; he is basically restating his disagreement.

The traditional story of man

The literature and poetry of the Christian tradition give an answer to the question 'What is man?' in the form of a story. Let us look at this story and then see how far it can stand up to reflective consideration in the twentieth century.

The story begins with Adam and we must remember from the beginning that 'Adam' has three meanings in Hebrew, which are cunningly interwoven in the Genesis story and which the original readers would all have been aware of. 'Adam' can be the name of an individual like 'John', it is a collective term meaning 'mankind' and it is a word that can mean 'earth' or 'ground' out of which Adam was made.

In a beautiful tale, we hear that Adam was created in innocence and in the image of God. However, he was not satisfied with his state and wished to be equal with God.[2] This led him to his first act of disobedience and through this, his fall from the perfection that he had been given. Then began man's wanderings and sufferings. But God had mercy and, in order to bring man back and eventually to restore him, he began to call forth a special people who would act as his messenger and be a light to the other nations and into which he could enter in a new and unique way in due time. So a faithful group is gathered. The Noah story is part of this process; the story of Abraham (who became the great symbol of faith in God's promise) another part. Eventually, under the leadership of Moses, a whole tribe is brought out of captivity and invited to enter into a special relationship or covenant with God. Man must keep God's law, especially its summary known as the Ten Commandments and, on his side, God will watch over and protect the tribe of Israel.

Then begins a new saga of wanderings and a new drama, for man still fails to be faithful, except in a few instances. The prophets call men back to God and give new insights into what God requires of man, but Israel stays rebellious even after the punishment of exile in Babylon, followed by yet another act of forgiveness when Israel returns to the promised land. Then comes the climax. After careful preparation, the image of God himself, the true Messiah, comes to be among the chosen people, not only offering forgiveness, but the possibility of life in communion with him. But, yet again, the greater part of the Jews refuse God's grace and Jesus is rejected and crucified. However, out of the faithfulness of Jesus and his followers a new Israel is born, which carries on the message of Jesus and represents him in the world.

All this is the essential story of man so far, but it has still to be completed. The meaning and purpose of life, according to this story, is for man to discover or rediscover both goodness and joy in union with God and in the communion of saints. When the time is ripe, this will be finally achieved, at least for all the faithful, and man's story, so far as this earth is concerned, will come to an end. Jesus will come again and all the redeemed will enter into eternal life.

Man and evolution

Such, in brief, is the traditional Christian story of man. It can be found in the Bible, in Milton, in Dante and in many other writings. We must now ask ourselves how far this story can be accepted in the light of intelligent reflection and an unblind faith. I suggest that in the light of what we now know about man from biology, anthropology and history, we can reinterpret the traditional story in a way that preserves its essential insights into the nature of man. Here is the story as I think that it can be retold, making use of the theory of evolution. This new story should not be seen as an alternative to the first story, but rather as an addition to it, or a commentary on it.

God, from the beginning of creation, purposed to make man. He intended to make a creature that would *voluntarily* respond to him and love him, that would be *responsible* for his brother and for animals and that would imitate his own creativity. But he would not, and I shall try to show could not, create such a creature in an instant. Man, if he is to correspond at all with our experience of him, must have an historical dimension. For example, each adult man and woman has a personal history in which he or she has actively participated in the achievement of character. If my character were simply 'put there' as part of me, in an instant act of creation, it would not be *my* character, for which I have some responsibility. If we realize that this historical dimension is essential to man, then there is a mistake in thinking that man *could* be created in an instant of time, for process is part of his nature. Further, just as we think of the individual person as evolving in the womb, it is much more natural to think of the human race as evolving through stages.

However, the evolution of man, which the Christian can see as the unfolding of a divine plan, does not proceed in a simple curve. There are stages which represent radical innovations, even if some kind of evolutionary explanation can be given for the change. For example, from the primeval sludge came life, in the sense of self-reproducing organic bodies. Whether or not scientists will one day be able to reproduce this step I do not know, but if they do so, it will not affect the essential point that I am making. The important thing is that with life we have a new *level* of being, a new kind of entity that requires new words and new categories of thought to describe. It is not simply that life is more complex (in a way it may be less complex than some non-living compounds), it is complex in a new *kind* of way.

But this is only the beginning. After life came the evolution of sensitive life, that is of animals that are conscious of and react to their environment through a complex nervous system. Next came self-conscious life and with it reflective thought, freedom of action, creative genius and sacrificial love. At each of these stages in evolution we find a new *level* of being which demands new words and new categories of thought. For example, *thought*, in itself, cannot be described, let alone explained, except in terms of mind, that is at the level of self-conscious awareness. A biologist's account of electrical energy in the brain may describe what accompanies thought, or what is the physical manifestation of thought, but not what thought *is*.

As we think of the different levels at which creatures exist, we should note that the possible existence of a kind of intermediate level is basically irrelevant. For example, some have argued that evolution is incompatible with Christianity because at some stage evolution demands semi-humans. But the Christian should be agnostic, in the strict sense of the term, on the subject of whether or not there were once such creatures. It is possible that there was a mutation jump to the first self-conscious human mating pair, in which case there would not have to have been any semi-humans, but it is not necessary for Christians to insist that this must have been the case. Why does it matter if there were intermediate beings at some stage, perhaps creatures who had occasional glimmerings of self-consciousness? (In other words, there is a difference of level between consciousness and self-consciousness, but there could be beings who lived partly at one level and partly at the other.)

In fact, Christian nervousness on this issue is largely based on the dogma that human beings have souls, but that animals do not, or, if they do, souls of a quite different kind. But although an absolute divide between animal and man is official doctrine in some churches, it is quite unnecessary for basic Christian doctrine. (I shall take up the question of the nature of the human soul again in chapter VIII.)

To return to the stages of evolution. If we stress the emergence of new levels, from matter to life to consciousness to self-consciousness, then far from evolution being an embarrassment for Christian faith, it can be seen as an aid. Not only is there compatibility between science and religion, but the idea of emergence illuminates the *spiritual struggle* which is an essential element in human life.

In order to see this, consider the following analogy. At some point in the evolution of life on this planet, there was a movement from the sea to the land. What probably happened is that some fish began to drag themselves on to the land and to spend part of their time there, either to avoid predators or to take advantage of food on the shoreline. No doubt these creatures were pretty uncomfortable out of the sea for they were in the process of emerging from one domain to another. The hybrid creature, half in the domain of sea and half in that of land, is an analogy for the state of man as he emerges from the animal world to the human world. In other words, the truly human level is not given, it has to be *achieved* as one chooses to try to live on the higher level. Evolution has produced a being with a nervous system that is capable of developing self-consciousness, freedom, love, etc., but all of these things have to be worked for as the new level emerges. In this struggle, the existence of intermediate positions, that is of those who are half animal and half man, is the order of the day, not the exception, but of course this is not quite the same thing as the semi-human we have just considered. The semi-human would have physiological limitations that prevented him from having more than glimpses of the human level. The half man of this paragraph is the creature who could be fully human, but who has failed in his spiritual struggle, or at least partially failed.

I could easily be misunderstood here. I am not saying that the animal level, that is the conscious but not self-conscious level, is bad. Far from it, for the Christian regards all the levels of creation as intrinsically good. The point is that the truly human or spiritual level (which I think are ways of referring to the same thing) is a higher level and one that all men are called to reach by a process that involves struggle (and, as we shall see, grace). Evil only enters the scene when some glimpse of the new level is seen and then rejected. Animals as such cannot be evil, only those with the capacity freely to choose a higher level of being. However, we may be agnostic on the question of whether some of the higher animals, other than man, can begin to transcend the strictly animal level. Once again, Christianity is not bound to a doctrine of an absolute division.

From all this we see that the discovery of personhood can only be achieved in an historical process in which a new level can emerge and only through the struggle of the creature that has the capacity for this level. Thus we do not find the doctrine of evolution a rival to the doctrine that God created man, but rather an illuminating comment on how he created man.

Original sin

While modern biology and anthropology pose no challenge to the basic doctrine of the creation of man in God's image, they do challenge the traditional doctrine of original sin. This must be faced squarely and, in my judgment, the outcome of any serious reflection is the demand that the ancient doctrine of original sin be reinterpreted (as indeed it has been by a number of modern theologians).

The classical doctrine, as commonly expounded, included the following elements: (1) there was an historical fall when the individual, Adam, was disobedient; (2) as a result all men are now born into a state of sin; (3) for this reason they inherit guilt at their birth which can only be dissolved by baptism (this is part of the reason for infant baptism); (4) this fall has profoundly affected man's sexuality, so that the lust which men and women have for each other is itself a sign of sin. Ideally, the procreation of children should be without this lust and it has often been claimed that the perfect Christian should abstain from all sexual activity. Hence the doctrine of the ever-virginity of Mary in some churches, which claims that Mary continued as a virgin for *all* her married life;[3] this must not be confused with the doctrine of the virgin birth. Hence, too, the 1950 encyclical in the Roman Catholic church which insists that the celibate state is intrinsically higher than the married state.[4]

It is doubtful whether much of this can stand up to rational criticism, especially the historical fall (given the fact that the Genesis story was written in symbolic form, not as history), the notion of inborn guilt[5] (when our ordinary morality insists that we must participate willingly in any act for which we can be held responsible) and the puritan doctrine of sex[6] (which most churches have rejected in the twentieth century).

However, having said all this, most contemporary Christians still feel that there is something true and important in the old doctrine of original sin if it is stated properly, so that element (2) above is separated from the other elements, and explained in a new way. The following points need to be stressed as true and important: (1) there is a universal or near universal fact of human moral failure (The chief reason for this failure is that we start life with an animal egoism, which, although not sinful in itself, invites all men to prefer selfish satisfaction to a response to the good. This animal egoism, I have tried to show, is the necessary *starting point* for *human* development.); (2) this moral failure is due not only to our individual weaknesses, but also to a social pressure that invites and encourages our failure, a pressure that comes from a sort of collective force of human evil that is there before we are born; (3) while we cannot inherit guilt, we can inherit responsibilities of a kind (not only to honour our parents, but also to right some of the wrongs that our parents or our culture have been responsible for). These are all fundamental truths and I shall argue in chapter XIII that part of the trouble with Marxism is its failure to understand them. In a somewhat confused way, the doctrine of original sin has always stood for them, but they have been mixed up with mumbo-jumbo that an unblind faith must purge (though a mumbo-jumbo that is historically understandable, for it looks back to the days before Jeremiah[7] when men believed in collective guilt as part of their primitive way of thinking).

On balance, I think that Christians should continue to refer to 'original sin', despite the misunderstandings that the term tends to cause, but insist that it refers to the three positive truths just mentioned and insist, too, that like many other truths it has been traditional to enshrine it in a myth. In this revised form, original sin is perfectly

27

compatible with evolution and with the other insights into the nature of man that have been provided by contemporary science.

The story of man and the story of Man

The view that man is by nature a creature *in process* and that moral and spiritual qualities have to be *achieved* rather than given, can be illustrated and supported by observing the similarity of the story of the individual man and the story of Man, or mankind.

One aspect of the analogy is the purely biological one. We have learned that the human foetus in its mother's womb goes through many of the stages that mankind has passed through as a species. For example, there is a fish-like stage that gradually gives way to a terrestial-like stage. It has always seemed odd to me that anti-evolutionists don't have any problem with the evolution of man in the womb, while they object to the evolution of Man in history. This is particularly odd in view of the fact that man is not perfectly formed, for example, his back is too weak for his upright posture, despite the common claim of fundamentalist preachers about our physical perfection. But this imperfection is completely explicable in terms of evolutionary theory.

However, there is another aspect to this analogy which is even more interesting and that is between the struggle of man and of Man in order to become human. The story of Man is one of a struggle to survive and then to flourish. He discovers that he can only survive as a species through social co-operation and the increasing use of his intelligence. The struggle is against the hardships of nature and the danger of fellow-man and also against the selfish or egotistical side of man's nature which struggles with his capacity to cooperate and to love. As we have seen, man's egoism is not *initially* evil, it is simply part of his animal nature and perhaps essential for his survival, but it becomes a source of evil when the private good, or rather the private apparent good, is preferred to the social good. This is the context for the moral and spiritual struggle of man, the result of which can be the emergence of something not formerly seen on this planet, namely moral character.

The point I am making here is that the last few sentences can apply equally to the story of mankind, or to the story of individual man or woman. In biblical language, the flesh fights against the spirit,[8] but the flesh is not evil in itself, it is only evil when chosen instead of spirit. Hence the word could become flesh.[9]

Thus the analogy between the story of man and the story of Man helps to indicate what man is and where he is going. Finally then, what can be said of the end of man or of Man?

The word 'end' in English has two meanings. It can mean 'end' in the sense of 'final stage', just as a station may be at the end of the line (here 'end' corresponds to the Greek word *eschatos*). It can also mean 'end' in the sense of 'purpose', just as we might say that the end of the railway was to make safer passage between two cities (here 'end' corresponds to the Greek word *telos*). In a Christian philosophy, there must be an end for man in both senses, but the second sense, that of *telos*, is the most crucial, for the Christian sees the whole creation as the product of a Mind that has a purpose for man. I shall take up the question of man's final end or purpose in chapter VIII.

IV Jesus is Lord

Jesus and God

The Christian will often hear a preacher say 'Jesus is God', or will be expected to sing hymns which refer to Jesus as 'Lord God Almighty'.[1] It may surprise some readers to hear that, strictly speaking, such phrases do not reflect traditional Christian doctrine. The idea of God, in itself, is of a being that transcends space and time, so that it could not be correct to say, *without qualification*, 'Jesus is God'. This would suggest that one could equally say 'God is Jesus' and that is certainly not Christian doctrine. Therefore, the official doctrine has always qualified claims about the divinity of Jesus and said 'Jesus is the son of God', or 'Jesus is the second person of the Trinity', or 'the Word was God', quoting St John.[2] The phrase which I prefer is that of St Paul when he describes Jesus as 'the image of the invisible God'.[3]

Why have Christians made such claims and what do they mean? It is especially important to answer these questions when we hear well-disposed critics of Christianity say, 'Why can't we just say that Jesus was a very good man, or one of the prophets, or even the greatest of the prophets?' I shall try to answer this question from the point of view of a Christian philosophy. This philosophy may not be one hundred per cent orthodox, but it is certainly a *Christian* view rather than a Humanist or Unitarian view and it is also one that I believe can be held with complete integrity by one who seeks an unblind faith. It is also compatible with either a Protestant or a Catholic emphasis. The first half of my answer involves an examination of the biblical account of the life of Jesus, and the second half, which is equally necessary, involves seeing the Christian doctrine of Christ within the context of an overall philosophy of God and man.

30

In chapter XII I shall tackle the question of the accuracy of the Bible, but for the time being let us work on the assumption that the New Testament, even if inaccurate in some matters of detail, does give a generally true picture of the life and character of Jesus and, in particular, of the stories that he told (which were the things most likely to be remembered with accuracy).

It is clear that Jesus saw his coming as a climax in the history of Israel. His parables claim that now is the crucial moment, the time of the coming of the bridegroom, of the gathering of the harvest, of the finding of treasure, of the drawing in of the net and so on. One parable is of particular interest in this connection, namely the parable of the vineyard as it occurs in the twelfth chapter of Mark. All of Jesus' hearers would know that he was telling the story of Israel, for the vineyard was a common symbol for the chosen people and Jewish coins sometimes used bunches of grapes to symbolize their country, just as some Canadian coins use a maple leaf. When the harvest is ready, the Lord of the vineyard sends his servants to collect the fruits, but they are rejected by the tenants and some are killed. Again, every hearer would have seen the point for the prophets were commonly referred to as the 'Lord's servants', the messengers who came to Israel in every age calling for the fruits of obedience and good deeds. Then the parable goes on: 'He had still one other, a beloved son; finally he sent him to them, saying, "They will respect my son". But those tenants said to one another, "This is the heir; come, let us kill him, and the inheritance will be ours." '

It is clear from this, and from the other parables, that Jesus did not see himself merely as one of the prophets, but as something more. His own preference for a title seems to have been the phrase 'son of man', but he also accepted Peter's suggestion that he was the Christ, the son of the living God.[4] 'Christ' in Greek is the same word as 'Messiah' in Hebrew and means the anointed one. It is evident that Jesus accepted this title and also that he interpreted it in a different way from many Jews, notably the zealots, who were looking for a political Messiah. His decision to ride a donkey into Jerusalem rather than a horse was probably a deliberate sign to the zealots of the nature of his Messiahship and his frequent use of the suffering servant theme from the prophet Isaiah reinforced this. The Messiah had come to rule, but in the hearts and minds of men, and his path was one of suffering and humiliation.

There are many further indications that Jesus saw himself as something more than just another prophet. There was his claim to be able to forgive sins, which shocked many of his listeners,[5] there was his claim to be able to revise the law that God gave to Moses, especially his rejection of the old law, 'An eye for an eye and a tooth for a tooth.'[6] (In passing we should note that when Jesus tells us, in his revision of the law, to turn the other cheek, he is referring to insults; he is not necessarily insisting on pacifism in all cases.) Another crucial passage occurs when the disciples of John come to ask whether he is the expected one and Jesus replies, 'Go and tell John what you hear and see.'[7] It is clear in the context that Jesus is referring to the signs that accompany the coming Messiah.

At this point, some writers would add the miracle stories as vital testimony to the nature of Jesus, but, from the point of view of the unblind faith that this book is seeking to describe, I think that this is a mistake. This is not because I do not accept some of the miracle stories, but because (a) they are among the most disputed passages of the New Testament and at this stage I want to base the Christian claim about Jesus on a foundation that does not depend on historical passages that can easily be challenged; (b) even if accepted, the miracles do not prove Christian claims about Jesus, for it may be the case that many holy people have performed miracles; and (c) Jesus himself seems to have played down the use of his miracles as evidence.[8]

Nor, at this point, do I wish to make use of the series of 'I am' statements recorded in St John's gospel, such as 'Before Abraham was, I am.'[9] The reason for this is that it is difficult to be sure how far these statements refer to the actual sayings of Jesus and how far they reflect a meditation by the author of the gospel on the meaning of the life of Jesus. I must not be misunderstood here. I am not saying that Jesus did not say these things; I am saying that for the seeker of an unblind faith they cannot be used as *primary evidence* for the nature of Jesus. I tend to think he may have said these things *because* I believe, on other grounds, that Jesus is the image of God. This is a much more rational approach than the one which uses these sayings as primary evidence, when they are open to such obvious objections.

Jesus and prophecy

It is clear that according to the most ancient tradition in the New Testament Jesus saw himself as the Messiah and as more than a prophet. But this is not enough for a Christian philosophy, for it must be asked, 'Could Jesus have been wrong in his assessment of his own mission?' and 'If Jesus were more than a prophet, what exactly was he?' In order to respond to these questions, we have to look beyond the New Testament, for the New Testament picture itself is being challenged. In this section, I shall begin to build up a Christian philosophy of the nature of Jesus by looking at the Old Testament context of the life of Jesus, for he claimed to fulfil its prophecies.

We must note that 'prophecy' can mean two things. One we can call 'crystal ball gazing' and refers to an attempt to see the future in a kind of vision of what *is* there to be seen; as if in the middle of reading a novel we were to glance at the last page to see the future that is laid out. The other kind of prophecy is a matter of proclaiming the meaning of things as they are now, sometimes with the implications for the probable future. The great prophets of the Old Testament were primarily prophets in this latter sense, that is they were 'spokesmen' or 'forthtellers' rather than 'foretellers'. No doubt there are some elements of the first kind of prophecy in some of their utterances,[10] but in general thoughtful people are very nervous about this kind of prediction, partly because the notion that the future is fixed in detail seems to conflict with our ideas of freedom and responsibility and partly because it lends itself to unprofitable speculation, for example, about exactly when the world will end. When this kind of prophecy is found we can think of it either as the indication of a probable outcome, or more radically, as a relic from a more primitive outlook that should be discarded.

We should note here that when Jesus prophesied the destruction of the Temple at Jerusalem,[11] this too can be seen as a prophecy of the 'forthtelling' kind. He was not 'crystal ball gazing', but seeing the natural outcome of the contemporary tension between the Romans and the Jews and, in particular, the probable result of the growth of the zealot party. His prophecy was a kind of political realism. It was not a case of 'This is what is laid down in the future', but 'This is how things are going to turn out if people continue their present policies.' It was the same kind of realism that led Jesus to predict his betrayal and death. Towards the end of his ministry it became clear to Jesus that Judas would be the betrayer, but not because Judas was destined from before his birth to betray Jesus.

The great Old Testament prophets had something of the same sensitivity to the meaning of events and the character of God that Jesus displayed. They saw that the Jews had been chosen, not for their own sakes, but to be 'a light to the nations'.[12] Gradually, therefore, the Jews had to be taught their role and the true nature of God. Again and again God had rescued Israel, sent them messengers and tried to draw them to himself. So the prophets, beginning to understand the character of God, looked forward to a time when God would complete the process he had begun when he had called Israel and they saw this as happening through a new deliverer, the Messiah, who would unfold God's plan. When we ask what this Messiah would be like, we see the dramatic insight of these later prophets, especially in the writings of Isaiah. These prophets began to understand the inevitability of suffering by the good and something of its redeeming quality when experienced in the right way and for the right end. So the coming Messiah was not to be a conqueror, like Joshua, but a suffering servant. Indeed, the implication is that this is the role for the whole of Israel, if they are to fulfil God's purpose for them. So we find in Isaiah, Jeremiah, Hosea, the author of Job and in several Psalms, a new sensitivity to human life and human needs and a new vision of the nature of God's love.

This is the context in which we must understand Jesus' claim to fulfil the prophets and the Christian claim that he died and rose again 'according to the scriptures'.

Jesus as logos

So far we have explored how Jesus saw himself and the prophetic tradition which he claimed to fulfil. To these insights, a Christian philosophy must add a universal context in which we see the role of Jesus in terms of world history and the meaning of all life. In this way, the Christian can explain why he takes his scriptures as central for the meaning of life, rather than the scriptures of some other religious tradition.

The Christian philosophy goes as follows. God is the Father of all mankind and he seeks man's fulfilment by encouraging him to love both his fellow-man and God. To this end, he speaks to man in many ways, of which the sayings of the prophets are but one. Whenever God expresses himself through the presentation of what is good, true, or beautiful, then we can speak of his 'word' to man. Once again, we are relying here on a human analogy because we communicate with each other most typically in words. However, while God's word can refer to any of a thousand ways in which he speaks to man, there is a specially appropriate sense in which his 'word' refers to the ultimate way in which he spoke to man within the history of his dealings with the Jews. In these dealings, we see him reaching down to man, stage by stage extending his love and compassion. But there is a logical climax to this process (using 'logical' to mean a consistency with a general pattern), for all of God's acts of love point to the possibility of an ultimate act of love in which God *identifies* with man, so far as it is possible for an eternal being to do so. Thus St Paul says, 'God was in Christ reconciling the world to himself'[13] and others have said, 'We see in Jesus, in time, the character of God in eternity.'

This way of looking at things, which sees Jesus as more than a prophet because he is the embodiment of an act of identification, involves going beyond the purely biblical context, for it relates to our experience of life as a whole. Each day, we see love and hatred and their effects and we see how the highest form of love between human persons involves an act of identification. In this act, sometimes we have to go literally 'where he was' in order to reach our friend, just as the good Samaritan had to go physically to the man in need, and it always involves a mental and spiritual identification with the friend or neighbour. This identification may involve physical suffering and it always involves spiritual suffering as we share another's burden (or spiritual joy as we share his happiness). It is this human experience of love, with its logical climax in acts of identification, that adds enormous significance to St John's assertion: 'And the word became flesh, and dwelt among us . . .'[14] Here the biblical tradition of God's love reaching down to man and the universal human experience of love come together. God expresses his love and shows us his word, in the most complete way possible within the conditions of this world.

The initiative of God

It must now be evident why it is so hard for the Christian to say precisely who Jesus was or is, and why, when he speaks of the nature of

Jesus he is bound to claim that we are dealing with a great mystery. A 'mystery' in the proper sense of the word is not a superstition. A mystery arises when human experience faces us with mind-boggling questions that we find ourselves compelled to ask, but which we are aware that we are incapable of answering adequately. Modern physics is full of such questions and so is religion. From the point of view of an unblind faith, there are no grounds for accepting the irrational, but there are grounds for making do with only partial answers to some of our fundamental questions.

With respect to the nature of Jesus, the mystery arises because the indications that we have explored in this chapter suggest a person who is truly a man (otherwise he cannot *identify* with mankind), but who is also, in some extraordinary way, a revelation of God. The theme that brings together this dual aspect of the nature of Jesus is that of the *initiative* of God in Jesus, an initiative that is indicated in all three of the contexts we have explored (Old Testament, New Testament and daily experience). If Jesus were simply a very good man, as is the belief of many non-Christians who have a profound respect for him, then what happens to this initiative? Perhaps it is not lost altogether, but essentially it is the same sort of initiative as can be seen when God is in contact with any prophet or saint. For example, on a humanistic interpretation, what happens to the Christmas story? It is still beautiful, but it only has significance because of what Jesus *became*, it cannot in itself be any more significant than the birth of any other baby boy or girl (though I certainly don't want to belittle the significance of that). But for the Christian the story has an enormous additional meaning, even if some of the details, such as the virginity of Mary, are pious myths rather than historical fact. (On such matters we may be agnostic and Christian at the same time.) The point is that here God takes a new and awesome step in the drama of his approach to men; he chooses to become as man, that we may become as God. He comes to share our humanity that we may share his divinity. As Athanasius put it, powerfully even though a little misleadingly, 'God made himself man, that man might become God.'[15]

No doubt such language is mysterious, but I have argued that it is not *totally* baffling for we have glimpses of what it means through our own experience. We know what it is to share with others, to take part in their joys and sufferings and in a sense to choose to be 'one' with them. Similarly, God chose to be 'one' with us and hence the mystery of Christ. Some of the ways in which Christians have attempted to describe this mystery will be examined in the next two chapters.

Jesus is Lord

The first Christians did not have a worked out formula for the nature of Jesus, but they had a creed, an extremely short creed that is frequently referred to in the Acts of the Apostles,[16] namely 'Jesus is Lord', or 'Christ is Lord'. (Christians tend to speak of 'Jesus' when they are thinking of the person whom they follow and 'Christ' when they think of his role, or the meaning of his life.) To assert this creed, plus genuine repentance, was all that was required of the first Christians at their baptism. This creed put on one side all sorts of complex questions about exactly how Jesus is related to God, but it affirmed that the believer accepted Jesus as his Lord, as the one he had to follow in order to find the true meaning of life. Jesus stood for the good, the true and the beautiful, and thus pointed man towards God.

In chapter IX, when we look at the essentials and the non-essentials of the Christian faith, I shall recommend a return to the use of this simple creed for many occasions. A person who doubts just about everything in traditional Christian theology, but who can say 'Jesus is Lord' with conviction, is a Christian in a real sense. He may not yet have developed a Christian philosophy, he may even have doubts about the reality of God, but this commitment puts him inside the circle of faith. This is the chief thing that binds all Christians together in one family over whom Christ is Lord.

V Jesus is Saviour

Jesus and superman

Gradually the central role of Jesus in a Christian view of the world is emerging. First we had to build an idea of a loving God who is seeking to reach down to man and call him to union with himself and his fellow man. Then we had to understand the essential nature of man and the emergence of his spiritual nature as he reaches up to God. Then we come to Jesus, who is a kind of bridge figure, who binds together within himself the principles of God and of man.

One way of drawing out the significance of Jesus for the Christian is to contrast him with 'superman' or with many of the other heroes that the young, and the not so young, of this generation are being presented with. Heroes like superman are basically irrelevant to our lives, not because they are imaginary, but because they share few, if any, of our human problems. In an emergency they can fly away, or call upon super-human strength, or magic. In contrast, the heroes of great literature share our human condition and we can be inspired by them even when they are imaginary. This applies even to fantasies like Tolkein's trilogy of the ring, where Boromir is tempted and falls and where even Gandalf has to fight the temptation to take and use the ring of power.

This illustrates the importance of the claim that Jesus was tempted, or tested, in all points like ourselves[1] and that he would not call angels to his aid[2] and indeed *could* not if he were to accept the full implications of taking on the human condition.[3] Thus he can inspire us because his life is relevant. He shared our condition and yet, we believe, lived in total obedience to the good, without sin. He had no special advantage in this respect and the view that he alone (except perhaps for Mary) was born without original sin is based on the old-fashioned view of that doctrine that we looked at in chapter III. When properly described, original sin is an aspect of the human social condition which Jesus fully shared with us and it does not mean that we *must* sin, by some absolute inevitability. The perfect man will be tempted (among other reasons because, like Jesus, he has the passions or drives that come with a human body), but with God's help it is possible not to sin.

Because of the way in which he shared our condition, Jesus is called not only lord, but saviour. This is in part a play on the name 'Jesus', which literally means 'saviour' in the Hebrew, and also refers to the claim that with his help we can be saved from sin and from the final death which is its result. The meaning of this claim will be explored in the rest of this chapter.

Sin and guilt

Both the Hebrew and the Greek words translated as 'sin' convey a series of ideas, but the central one is of 'falling short of the mark', like an arrow that fails to reach its target. Thus sin, in its primary sense, is the voluntary choice of something less than the good. It refers both to many of the acts and to the condition of all or almost all men and women once they have reached years of discretion. Because of the pressure of our culture and of our fellow men, sin has a frightening element of predictability about it. Nevertheless, I stress again that it is a voluntary matter, otherwise we can make no sense of God's judgment and of our responsibility. If, at any moment, a man cannot choose the good, or at least the lesser evil, perhaps because of a chemically or physically damaged brain, then the question of sin cannot arise. What is inevitable and predictable, given the myriad occasions and the nature of the forces at work, is that sooner or later most men will sin.

The effect of sin is the destruction of what is truly human, if by 'human' we mean what man can become when he responds to the good, the true and the beautiful. It distorts or destroys the process of emergence from the animal level. Man does not then return to the animal level, for this in itself is natural and sinless, but he sinks to a level below it. Paradoxically, his own egoism then gets him caught up in a selfishness which destroys the possibility of anything beyond a superficial happiness, for true happiness depends on relationships of love with others that cannot coexist with selfishness. Worse still, this selfishness becomes a sort of disease that feeds on itself as one sin leads on to another.

39

Guilt is the appropriate sentiment for someone who knows that he has sinned. Contrary to what some psychologists say, there is nothing essentially neurotic about guilt; the problem is that many people feel guilty about the wrong things. For example, Victorian boys and girls were taught to feel guilty about their adolescent sexual dreams and fantasies, which were mostly perfectly natural and were either sinless, or sinful in a very low degree. At the same time, they were not generally taught to feel guilty about the intense suffering caused when they bullied an unpopular class-mate. But here, I maintain, feelings of guilt would be highly appropriate. Similarly, many of us may have neurotic guilt feelings, but usually it is not the guilt itself that is neurotic, it is the lack of judgment about where and when we should feel it.

One other aspect of sin must be stressed here. We are not only responsible for our voluntary actions; in the long run we are also responsible for many sides of our character. Even in the fourth century BC Aristotle saw that this must be so if we are to be able to give an adequate account of the moral life, for otherwise we could simply blame many of our bad actions on our temper or moodiness. Similarly, good actions would not be the result of *virtue*, but mere consequences of character.[4] No doubt some aspects of our character are purely genetic and Aristotle calls these 'natural dispositions', in contrast with real virtues,[5] but by the way we choose to act now we form habits which gradually develop into our genuine virtues and vices. If adults have bad tempers, they are at least partially to blame.

Atonement

One of the great insights of the Christian faith is the recognition that, in the face of sin, self-help is not enough. Human effort is certainly demanded, but by itself it eventually leads to despair. Indeed, in an odd way, the very struggle to improve the self tends to turn in upon itself and intensify the concern with *myself*. Further, when there is some success in the struggle, pride in this success tends to follow.

However, some people, both Christian and non-Christian, can and do transcend this vicious circle of egoism and achieve a level of selfless-ness. This is part of our human experience and we see it happen when-ever people love. I am not primarily talking about 'falling in love' in a romantic way, though this too is a beautiful thing that often includes love in its richest sense, but love for one's friends and, if relationships are as they should be, love for parent or child. We are all capable of this love and when we experience it we are in some degree drawn out of our selfish centres and others become as central and important in our eyes as we are ourselves.

The origins of this capacity to love are probably there in the evolutionary process. For a species to survive, it often became necessary that members should sacrifice themselves for others. For example, we can see in nature how a mother bird may deliberately sacrifice herself when a bear climbs the tree towards the nest where the fledglings lie. Thus the cynical suggestion that man *can* only act selfishly (for example, for the sake of gaining heaven, or being well thought of, or appeasing his own conscience) is a mistake. Along with many other animals, we have evolved with both ego drives and species drives and the latter look to the good of the group, or at least to the good of one's kin. The development of morality depends upon building on this species drive that is already there within us. But, just as in general the emergence of the human order involves a *new level* of being, so here, in man's moral life, a quality of love can emerge which goes beyond the species drive. The poetry of love, including the thirteenth chapter of I Corinthians is abundant evidence of this.

Thus love is the answer to sin and guilt and to the selfishness that underlies them. It is important to see that the Christian doctrine of forgiveness and atonement (in which we become 'at one' with God and fellow man) is based on this universal human experience of love, only it is raised to a universal teaching about human salvation and based on a spectacular outpouring of God's love. The Christian claim is that in Christ is symbolized the truth of how man can discover his true end and, moreover, that in Christ there occurred in history a divine action which transformed the situation caused by man's sin. The prodigal son can return home as a son because the father has reached out to meet him.

The symbolic meaning of Christ's work is not hard to see. St Paul put it like this: 'As in Adam all die, even so in Christ shall all be made alive.'[6] Adam symbolizes raw man, that is man struggling to emerge from the animal level but failing to achieve his potential. Christ represents the new man, the new creation, the image of what man can be and shall be. But when we seek to go beyond the symbolism and ask, 'How does this divine initiative actually help man?', what can we say?

41

Although we cannot fully understand the mystery of Christ's work, we are not asked blindly to accept it as a fact. Once again we can strive for an unblind faith and in the next two sections I shall show how we can begin to grasp the significance of what Jesus did.

The power of love

The first way in which we can begin to *understand* the work of Christ is to appreciate the power of example and the way in which a demonstration of love can draw out a response that would not otherwise have been possible. So, looking at the results of the life of Jesus, St John said, 'We love, because he first loved us'[7] and this effect seems to have been anticipated by Jesus himself when he said, 'I, when I am lifted up from the earth, will draw all men to myself.'[8]

Here is one of the many places where there is harmony between the teaching of the Bible and our contemporary experience of human life. For example, A does an injury to B out of anger or malice, but quite unexpectedly B does not retaliate when he could, but offers a creative solution to the quarrel. At this point A faces a new opportunity. He may reject the hand of friendship, or (and most of us have seen this happen) he may accept it and out of the quarrel can emerge peace and reconciliation.

In the above example, it matters that the person showing love actually demonstrates it in a particular event or set of events. Similarly, if man is to know the love of God with all the power that actual examples can have, then there has to be an actual event or set of events in which man sees the love of God. This, Christians believe, is the meaning of the cross. In one sense, the cross transcends time, for it demonstrates an eternal principle, that is of the lengths to which God's love will go; but for man's sake this love had also to be acted out in an historical event. Because of this event, man can respond in a way which would not otherwise have been possible, for the demonstration of love calls forth a response of love. Henceforth, man can serve Jesus as Lord not for his own ends, not even for the sake of heaven[9] (the search for which can easily be a long-run variety of selfishness), but purely as a response to God's love. When we love, we do not need an additional motive, the other becomes for us an end in himself or herself.

In stressing the power of the example of Jesus, we must not look at the cross in isolation from the rest of his life. If we do, there tends to follow a morbid concentration on blood and sacrifice and a magical theory of the atonement in which an angry God is somehow appeased by the offer of a sacrificial lamb. There is, indeed, great symbolic power in this notion of the sacrificial lamb, but in the hands of many fundamentalist preachers it is taken so literally that we end up with absurdity, as if blood in itself had any power, or as if the righteousness of Christ could be transferred to us in a quasi-mechanical exchange. To believe in the atoning power of the work of Christ does not involve having to accept dubious theories that do violence to our rationality and our morality. God did indeed achieve reconciliation, not by magic, but through an extension of the power of love that we see all around us.

When we emphasize the cross in the context of a whole life, then we see that the particular manner of Jesus' death is secondary. The crucial thing is that, in being faithful to his identification with man, it was inevitable that sooner or later he would be violently rejected. We may recall that Plato had prophesied, in the true sense of prophecy that we have referred to, that a perfect man would eventually be put to death.[10] Jesus had to live as a man, not as a superman or as an angel dressed up as a man, and he had to live through this act of identification to the end.

Some radical Christians would go even further than I have here and suggest that even if Jesus had died of measles, or some other disease that happened to be man's enemy at the time, it would have made no difference, for this too would have been the acceptance of the human condition with no strings attached. Others claim that the symbolic power of the crucifixion is such that providence steered the inevitable death to take this form. I leave readers to reflect on this suggestion for themselves.

One further reflection on the power of love is appropriate at this point. In human relationships, one of the most powerful forces is the acceptance of people as they are. For example, in true friendship, we love the friend as he or she is and not as we think that they ought to be. The result is that one does not have to act a part in the presence of one's true friends, as if one were in danger of losing their affection. Again, one of the most powerful elements in the stability of family life, at its best, is the fact that children feel a loving acceptance, not for the gifts or virtues that the parents would like to see, but simply for themselves. Similarly, those who are seeking God can find an incredible sense of relief and of joy in the realization that God loves them as they are. As

Jesus put it, he came to call the sinners, not the righteous.[11] Thus one Christian writer has expressed the heart of the Christian message as the call to 'accept that we are accepted'.[12] The same note is sounded in the hymn 'Just as I am, without one plea . . . O Lamb of God, I come.'

Life 'in Christ'

When we consider the achievement of Christ, the power of the example of Jesus does not exhaust the meaning of his life when seen as an historical event. Another crucial result of his coming is the opening up of a new kind of participation or union with others 'in Christ'.

For some readers this will seem a very strange idea, so let us begin its exploration outside the Bible and then return there, in order to see how yet again the Christian view is one that completes or fulfils something found in everyday experience.

Suppose that we ask how far our true nature lies in our private individuality and how far it lies in a merger with a group or whole. On this issue, a traditional Christian philosophy steers a middle course. The purely individualistic life is incomplete and lonely and yet the opposite extreme, where there is to be a merging of ourselves with a whole in which we altogether lose our individuality, also seems to be a mistake, even though it is the express goal of some religions which speak of our souls being absorbed into the great Soul, like a drop into the ocean. If such is to be the final end of man, what is the purpose of the creative activity which brings forth such variety and the wonder and beauty of individual characters? Thus a compromise is suggested. True human living involves transcending our egotistical view of the individual person and seeing our very life as being bound up with the lives of others, with whom we share joy and sadness, but in a relationship in which there is still an 'I' and a 'you'.

This is the place to bring in the proper use of the word 'mysticism'. In popular usage, this word often refers to anything mysterious or odd, but, properly used, it refers to an important and specific type of experience that is found in all the great religions, the experience described as union with God. Whatever we make of experiences of this kind, they are in one sense facts, at the psychological level. As I have pointed out in the case of the experience of the numinous, which has something in common with the experience of union, one of the grounds for taking religion seriously is the fact that different people in many times, places and religions, have described very similar experiences. Sometimes the account is of a person becoming literally one with God, in a kind of organic union. In other accounts, the description suggests that there is a joy caused by a close relationship with God, in which there is still a self that is distinct from God's being. For mystics who use the second kind of language, an analogy for union with God is often sought in the union of two human lovers, as in the Song of Solomon. How we should interpret these accounts is a fascinating and difficult question, but all that I want to do here is to re-emphasize that there is a general human experience of life in communion, in which our true selves are found only in the context of a fellowship in which the very core of our being is transformed through our relationship with God and with others.

We can now turn to the biblical expression of this strata of human experience. It is strongly emphasized in the teaching of Jesus. For example, consider his statement, 'Unless a grain of wheat falls into the earth and dies, it remains alone; but if it dies, it bears much fruit. He who loves his life loses it . . .'[13] This expresses the theme briefly and brilliantly, for it is precisely the solitary state, the remaining 'alone' that is the cause of the real death of the person. We should also recall the last conversations between Jesus and the disciples as recounted in St John's gospel. Even if these are meditations on Jesus' life rather than his actual words, it is reasonable to assume that they reflect what the author had learned from Jesus. Of particular interest is the passage 'You will know that I am in my Father, and you in me, and I in you', followed by 'I am the vine, you are the branches.'[14] To these sayings we must add the recurring theme of St Paul's letters concerning life 'in Christ'. This is the new level of being that he and the other Christians had come to experience and which was symbolized in the baptism which indicated that one died, lived and rose again, with Christ and 'in Christ'.[15]

The principal reason for the shallowness of so much contemporary church life and for the boredom which accompanies so many church services and meetings is that this life 'in Christ' is not the living experience of the ordinary churchgoer. It is either unknown, or merely an interesting *idea*. But for those who can recapture the living experience, we have here the principal clue to an understanding of how Jesus' coming, in a unique historical event, can open up a path to salvation. Just because he became man, we can enter into a new kind of union with him in which the whole level of our being is raised. 'No man is an island'[16] in so far as he has discovered what being a person is really about. This discovery, as I have shown, is indicated in our daily experience of love and friendship and it is spotlighted and brought to fulfilment in the mystical experience of the saints in all the great religions. The work of Christ takes on a new dimension of meaning when we see it in this context, for what he did was to open up to all of us the possibility of a new life in union with him.

VI Father, Son and Holy Spirit

Reason and paradox

The doctrine of the Trinity represents the most baffling part of the church's teaching for many thoughtful Christians. In this chapter, my purpose is not to make the idea of the Trinity clear and simple, for that would be as absurd as trying to give a simple yet adequate account of the nature of God. My purpose is: (*a*) to indicate that the doctrine is not there for the sake of bafflement, but represents human attempts to grapple with some fundamental aspects of our experience; and (*b*) to give an initial insight into the meaning of the doctrine.

A rational approach to man's fundamental questions does not always demand that we be able to understand all things, but that we stretch our rational faculties as far as we can and that we only accept paradoxes when they seem to be forced upon us by the need to be faithful to different aspects of experience. We recall that we are looking for an unblind faith, one that is neither blind acceptance nor a demand that we be able to comprehend all things. To put this in another way; there is one kind of paradox that we should be prepared to entertain, namely one that is not a contradiction as such, but one which we believe *appears* as a contradiction because of our limited viewpoint and which arises out of our attempts to explain things that our minds can only begin to grasp. In modern physics there are many examples of this, some with regard to the origins of the universe, some that arise when objects approach the speed of light, some that arise in the discussion of black holes and so on. In the light of the paradoxes that physics has to produce at this stage of its growth, we have no grounds for objecting in principle when religious thought faces paradoxes in its search for the origin and nature of the universe from its own perspective. What reason demands in this kind of inquiry is that we only accept paradoxical statements when they are forced upon us by our very attempt to be rational.

Trinity and tritheism

Unfortunately, the doctrine of the Trinity is one of the least understood of Christian doctrines. I recall a discussion with an intelligent Muslim who had attacked the Christian faith because of its belief in the Trinity. I asked him what he understood by the doctrine and he then explained it as if it were a crude tritheism, that is a belief in three separate Gods who are somehow united. His response indicated that, as so often happens, he was attacking something he had not really understood. This is rather like the situation that arises when people condemn books that they have not read, but my Muslim friend had much more excuse because many Christians themselves tend to talk of the Trinity as if it were a kind of tritheism, like the preachers I have already criticized who say simply and without qualification, 'Jesus is God'.

Part of the misunderstanding of the Trinity, and a factor that has led to it being confused with tritheism, lies in the use of the word 'person'. Almost every reader will know that in Christian teaching it is said that there is one God in three persons, the person of the Father, the person of the Son and the person of the Holy Ghost (though recently the word 'Spirit' has tended to be used instead of the more archaic 'Ghost'). When the doctrine was first formed, this was a reference to the Latin word *persona* (and the Greek *hypostasis*), the primary meaning of which is not 'person' in the modern English sense, but 'mask'. In the ancient theatre it was normal for the actors to put on masks, in which way they formally took on a role. Thus the original language of the Latin and Greek formulations of the doctrine of the Trinity was much less likely to suggest three separate entities, but pointed rather to one actor who played three different roles as he wore three different masks. However, this last description must not be taken any more literally than the idea of three separate beings, for when an actor takes off one mask he puts on another, while in the Christian doctrine the three masks or 'personae' of God represent permanent aspects of his nature.

For the present, let us make use of the idea of three *aspects* of God, inadequate as even this approach is, and look at the experiences of God in the Bible that have led to emphasis on these three aspects. Then, as elsewhere in this book, we shall try to relate this biblical experience to our general experience of life.

Father, Son and Holy Spirit

In the Old Testament, the word 'Father' is not normally used in reference to God until we come to the later books and then only twice in the form of a prayer.[1] In Jesus' teaching, however, 'Father' is the usual word for the God of Israel who had spoken to Abraham, Moses and the other prophets and who had led the Jews to the promised land. When we look back from the New Testament to the use the word 'God' in the Old Testament, there is no doubt that if we are to use one of the words, 'Father', 'Son', or 'Spirit', it would normally be the word 'Father' that would be most appropriate, as Jesus' custom confirms. The aspect of God that is central in this usage is the idea of God as creator and sustainer of all beings other than himself. One example of a passage that powerfully evokes a sense of this creator-source of the universe is the great nature psalm with its climax in the verse 'O Lord, how manifold are thy works: in wisdom hast thou made them all; the earth is full of thy riches.'[2] In modern writings, the hymn 'This is my father's world' expresses the same theme. Closely associated with this sense of the creator-source is that of the numinous. This, as we have seen, is an intense feeling of an awesome majesty, beyond and within all things. One example that clearly reflects such a sense is the passage which describes Isaiah's vision in the temple and the words 'Holy, holy, holy is the Lord of hosts'[3] spoken by the seraph.

If we are asked to indicate passages in the Bible where the Son aspect of God is revealed, the obvious answer for the Christian is in the life and teaching of Jesus. This answer, of course, is based on the ideas expressed in chapters IV and V and on the general conclusion that Jesus is the Son of God. However, even within the context of the Bible, this reference to the physical life of Jesus does not exhaust the idea of the Son, for the New Testament writers claimed that Jesus did not come into being at his birth, nor even at his conception, but that in some sense he had always existed. The incarnation marked a new identification with humanity, not the very beginning of his existence. This pre-existence of Jesus is implicit in the very idea of the word, or *logos*, that became flesh and it is quite explicit in the Epistle to the

Hebrews where the Father is said to have made the world *through* the Son.[4] However, although from the point of view of theology the eternal Son is prior to the actual events of Jesus' life, from the point of view of human experience, it is the knowledge of Jesus Christ, as the image of God, that comes first. Hence, while 'Father' refers primarily to the aspect of God as creator-source, 'Son' refers to the image of God as seen in Jesus. Here God, in a sense, is made concrete, so that we can see his character in time and space.

The idea of the 'Spirit' of God pervades both Old and New Testaments and it always refers to a divine energy or power, often manifested in the here and now. Jesus used the analogy of the wind, with its power and unpredictability, to describe Spirit: 'The wind blows where it wills . . . but you do not know whence it comes or whither it goes.'[5] At Pentecost, perhaps the most dramatic of all the experiences of the Spirit, it seemed to be both like wind and like fire.[6] When people feel the power of God actually at work within them, they tend to talk of the Spirit. Thus it is said that the Spirit came upon Samson whenever he was filled with power[7] and in true prayer we sense the Spirit of God somehow actually within us, helping us to pray.[8]

This idea of God within us must be stated carefully. In some religions, notably orthodox Hinduism, the central core of each person is literally a part of God, part of his Spirit. Some Christians have described their sense of God within them in the same language, but orthodox Christianity has always denied that God's Spirit is *identical* to ours, rather it can be in a union with ours that assists and encourages our individual spirits. We have the same situation here that I described with respect to mystical experience in the last chapter, where the Christian interpretation of mystical experience is of a union that still respects our individuality. But this universal sense of a God somehow actually at work *within* us is of such immense power that it must be understood as one of the foundations of all religion. Spirit, therefore, refers to that aspect of God which is known as a pervasive power that can invade the innermost recesses of our person.

Here, then, we have the three aspects of God as recorded in the biblical experience of man: three kinds of experience each of which the Christian has wanted to say are experiences of God himself. This is the biblical foundation for the claim that we know God in three persons.

The Trinity and human experience in general

This section is probably the most difficult part of this book, but I ask the reader to bear with me because there can be no easy treatment of this theme and yet its implications and importance are immense. In particular, I want to dispel some of the simplistic, tritheistic views of God that are held by many Christians and to show that an unblind faith is moved by serious reflection on the nature of God towards some kind of trinitarian doctrine.

The attempt to relate the Trinity to our general experience is not original; in fact, the claim that the Trinity is actually prefigured in human experience is a fundamental one in St Augustine. Among other analogies, he uses that of human love.[9] When we love another, there is the I that loves, there is the beloved that is loved and there is the love itself that is a kind of bond between the lover and the beloved. But truly there is only one thing here, namely love, and yet without these three elements there is no manifestation of love. Perhaps an even more helpful analogy is provided by the human mind itself and this is a particularly appropriate analogy if we stress the cailm that man is made in the image of God. Augustine too suggests an analogy based on the human mind,[10] but I am going to develop it in a way that is rather different from his.

When we think of man, there is a kind of trinity in the ideas of body, mind and spirit, that comprise him, but this is *not* the trinity that I am thinking of because it is possible to conceive of at least two of these elements separately. (Whether or not a human mind can exist without a body is a difficult question, but the fact that many, including Plato, believe that it can, makes these three ideas unsatisfactory as a model for the Trinity. It is essential for true trinitarianism that the elements be *inseparably* linked.) Instead, the model that I want to explore is based on the act of seeing. Here, there is an I, an object perceived, and the actual experience of perception, say the seeing of a tree. No human act of seeing can take place without all three of these elements, yet there is *one* experience, that in which an object is seen. Next, we must note that none of these elements can exist alone. The I only has meaning in the context of the awareness of something. (There is a sense in which the mind is aware of itself, but this can only arise because the mind is also perceiving things outside of itself.) Meanwhile, the object, conceived simply in itself, dissolves into a cloud of subatomic particles, which in turn dissolve into a cloud of formulae: it is only an *object* in the act of being seen. The redness, hardness and all the other qualities that we regard as substantial only arise in the context of perception. As for the third element, the perception itself, it is manifest that this demands both an I and an object.

The above is a very brief summary of an important and fascinating area of reflection and the reader can work through the issues more thoroughly in his own reading and reflection if he so chooses. However, it should be clear that the common view in which an I, or real subject, faces a substantial object, which somehow sends out rays to my eye whereby I can see it as it really is, is naive. In every act of seeing, the complex set of data that is coming to me from the object is interpreted and structured so that the act of seeing *any* thing is not the result of just opening my eyes and passively receiving what the object has to show. Rather perception is an active affair, in which one experience is made possible by three elements. There is an I, in the sense of an active mind that structures or processes all information it receives; there is something out there, a reality other than myself; and these two elements come together in the actual seeing, which we can describe as the spiritual *activity* of the person. This is what happens in any act of seeing and it is equally the situation in any other act of perception, such as hearing or feeling with the hands.

It should now be possible to see more clearly what the Trinity really stands for and why even the idea of three *aspects* of God is inadequate. It appears that the mind's knowing is not to be described in terms of a separate self that comes to know an object that is also quite independent of it, but as an *active process*. So it must be, the Christian claims, with God's knowledge, or with God's love, if we are to use the words 'knowledge' and 'love' with any meaning. However, there is also an important difference. In this case, it is not that God's awareness must be primarily of an object outside of himself, that is of the created order, for the Christian believes that God has a certain completeness in himself and that creation was a voluntary act. So if God is Mind and Love, which seem the most appropriate of all the descriptions of God, then there must be *activity* within the very nature of God himself.

The analogy of the three elements in the human mind can now be used as follows. The creator-source, that is the Father, eternally loves, not only in some abstract way, but with an actual object of his love called the eternal Son, the image of his nature. Within this image is also the idea of nature, or of anything else that the Father is free to create and which he will then love. But then we can also think of the act of love itself, called the Spirit, which binds together the Father and the Son just as the act of seeing binds together the subject and the object of seeing. It is only in this act of knowing or of loving, parallel to the act of perception in man, that anything is made actual or concrete. Thus, while we can properly say that the Father and the Son love, the love itself is most properly applied to the Spirit. Hence St Augustine said, 'The Holy Spirit is specially called by the name of love, although in the universal sense both the Father and the Son are love.'[11]

The realization that reflection on the Trinity is rooted in our own mental experience should help to carry us a long way from primitive tritheism. The stress is on the unity of the act of seeing and the unity of the divine knowledge and love. At the same time, there cannot be seeing, knowledge, or love, without these inter-related elements. This has been seen by many people in different ways. For example, the novelist Dorothy Sayers has a fascinating way of relating the writer's creative work to a trinitarian experience[12] and Hegel saw the unfolding of all reality in a trinitarian way, in which concrete reality must be the realm of Spirit.[13] We could go on, but it is clear that once again a fundamental Christian claim is not merely a biblical or ecclesiastical dogma, it is something rooted in human experience.

The Trinity and the Bible

Strictly speaking, the doctrine of the Trinity is not a biblical doctrine, for it is nowhere explicitly stated. The Christian claim is rather that the experience of God as found in the Bible, when reflected upon, demands such a doctrine.

Even in the Old Testament, there are suggestive passages where the ideas of the Spirit of God, or the Word of God, or the Wisdom of God, seem to be based on the insight that there are active relationships within God and yet not between *parts* of God. The tendency here, as with the Greek religion of the same period, was to set up notions such as 'Wisdom' as semi-independent entities, with an undefined status.[14]

As we saw in the third section of this chapter, the New Testament describes two principal experiences that lead on to trinitarian thought. First, there is the experience of Jesus of Nazareth and, for the reasons outlined in chapters IV and V, the Christian came to believe that here was more than a prophet but rather some new initiative of God. This led to the view that Jesus was in some unique sense the image of God and then to the further view that Jesus represented a word of God that had been there from all eternity. The incarnation was the making concrete, in terms of human nature, of a principle that was eternally true. This is the perfect image that God loves. Second, there is the overwhelming experience of the Spirit, both in its initial outpouring at Pentecost and in the individual experiences of many believers, especially at the moment of baptism.[15] Here was the reality and power of God within our very beings, rising up like an overflowing well of pure water, cleansing and enriching our souls.

I have already suggested that part of the trouble with contemporary Christianity is that many churchgoers do not know the 'in Christ' experience as a living reality. Another way of making the same point is to note how few Christians have undergone the Pentecostal experience. However, we must be very careful here because I do not want to suggest that Christians should all have the same *psychological experience* as the first Christians, for people are very different in this respect. Some contemporary Christians certainly do have the full Pentecostal experience and describe it in the same terms as did the first Christians; such people are often called the 'twice-born'.[16] Others, who may equally know the Holy Spirit within them, do not undergo this kind of experience; these are often called the 'once-born'. The former have to be very careful not to try to force the latter into their own mould, for God may have different roads for different people.

Thus the point of the last paragraph is not that we must all try to make sure that we have the same kind of Pentecostal experience, but that without a living experience of the power of the Spirit, as known either by the twice-born or the once-born, it is very hard to appreciate the transforming power that underlies trinitarian thinking. Here, in actual experience, is a kind of present or concrete reality, in which the presence of God is known. The creative source of the universe, made known to us in Jesus, is found as a living power within us. Here God is three and he is one.

The Trinity and the creeds

By now it should be apparent what the creeds are and what they are not. They are attempts to formulate the Christian insight into words, but they are not the directly revealed words of God, nor a simple statement taken out of the Bible. In my view, they can be subject to change and modification, though I would not like to see them altered without the joint approval of the major branches of the church, Orthodox Roman Catholic, Anglican and so on. The reason for this is that, with one exception, the present formulations of the Apostles' creed and of the Nicene creed were agreed upon by the majority of Christians in the early centuries and, inadequate as they may be, they do tend to bind the churches together. Moreover, the inadequacies of the creeds are basically irremovable because they lie in the inadequacy of human language and human analogy to express the full truth.

For these reasons, provided that the individual Christian can sympathize with the central ideas that underlie the doctrine of the Trinity, I do not believe that he or she should be overly worried about the actual phrases. They are *attempts* to express Christian convictions and they need interpretation. (For example, it is not of crucial importance whether or not Mary was a virgin in the strictly physiological sense. Again, we can be free to interpret Jesus' descent into hell either literally, or as a reference to his *spiritual* suffering on the cross.) At the same time, on the positive side, we can also exalt in the creeds, as patriots can do in a traditional song, and as I often do when I hear the liturgy sung in a Greek Orthodox church filled with people. Here, however inadequately, fellow Christians unite in expressing fundamental convictions. Most of the language may be obscure for the simple Greek villager, but he can still feel the power of the words as he participates in an ancient act and enters into a tradition that is still alive and which expresses the way Christians see God and his relation to us.

I mentioned 'one exception' to the unity of the churches in the creeds and this ought to be explained. One of the positive aspects of the creeds is the way in which they express the idea of movement or dynamic activity within God. Although Jesus was born as a man at a particular time, the Son, representing the principle of God's word, is not born, but is said to be 'eternally begotten'. This language seeks to express the view that, in terms of the three persons of the Trinity, there is a certain priority in that of the Father, but it is not a temporal priority for both are eternal. The Son, as it were, flows from the Father, as a river continually flows from a lake at its head-waters. Similarly, it is said that the Spirit 'proceeds' from the Father, again giving an idea of movement that has no beginning and no end. The Western church added the claim that the Spirit also 'proceeds' from the Son (in the famous *filioque* clause, which is the Latin for 'and from the Son'), thereby departing from the creed that had been approved by both Eastern and Western churches. The rights and wrongs of this particular issue would take us way beyond the scope of this book, but the controversy helps to explain the most important split within the Christian church. Also, it helps us to see clearly that the creeds are not the unalterable words of God, but human attempts to express the inexpressible.

In concluding this section, I want to make a suggestion with regard to how to teach the Trinity to children, for the approach taken in this chapter is obviously too advanced for them when they are small. I suggest that, in the early stages of Christian teaching, children should be taught that we have known God in three ways and that these correspond to aspects of God that are rather like the three sides of a pyramid. The biblical and general experiences of God as creator, of the man Jesus and of the sense of God's power within, can then be dwelt on. Then the young must be made to learn that their ideas must *grow* along with their growth in body. In the first instance, this can be applied to a richer understanding of prayer, with less emphasis on asking for things and more on our relationship with God. After this, young Christians can come to see that the pyramid with three sides is a very imperfect model for the nature of God and that if we take seriously the claim that God is 'Love' or that God is 'Mind', then either the trinitarian formula, or something that is generally equivalent to it, is inevitable. The Muslim, or the Unitarian, who denies the doctrine of the Trinity, has the very laudable intention of stressing the unity of God, but he does this at the expense of ignoring some of the issues that have to be faced in any talk of God as Love or Mind. It is all very well simply to insist that God is Love or that God is Mind, but *these assertions cannot actually mean anything* except within a doctrine that sees dynamic principles and activity within God. This is especially evident if we can say 'God is Love' or 'God is Mind' before, or apart from, the universe which he loves and knows. Christian philosophy has had the courage to see the implications of the claim that God is Love and that God is Mind.

How can we use words to describe God?

I want to end this chapter by returning to a question raised in chapter II which bothers many people when they start to think about the idea of God. How can we say anything that is true about God when we see something of the awesome majesty of God and the poverty of our language in this context?

Part of the answer has already been given. Christians believe that God has chosen to show himself to man, so that it is not simply a case of man striving to reach upwards towards the infinite. Further, if man is made in the image of God, then the principal way in which God shows himself is through men and women, when they are at their best. In addition to this stress on revelation, we have seen how language can be used *analogically*, that is when we stretch words so that we can begin to describe things that we only grasp dimly. We need to use language in this way in literature and science as well as in religion.

A further point about religious language can now be made in the light of the last few chapters. Some of the words that we use to describe God have a special relevance and suitability, in particular 'love', 'awareness' (mind), 'creativity' and 'freedom'. In all of these cases, although God has infinitely more of each quality than does man, so that we are still using analogies of a kind, in an important sense what God has more of is *the same thing*.

Take the case of the word 'freedom'. I have argued that even though man evolved, there is a gap, or difference of level, that emerges with man. There may be intermediate beings in the sense of semi-humans or animals that have flashes of self-awareness and freedom, but a glimpse of freedom is a glimpse of something *new*, just as the first photon of light to hit a dark screen is the first glimmer of light where before there was *no* light.

The nature of light provides a useful analogy for the phenomenon of consciousness. If one points a telescope at a very distant star, the light that is received comes, as it were, in packages, so that instead of measuring on an infinite scale, one counts photons. Moreover, one cannot measure less than a certain quantity of light; there cannot be half a photon. My suggestion is that, just as there is a radical difference

57

between light and no light (in the extreme case between counting one photon as a kind of blip on a screen and counting nothing), so there is a radical difference between being aware at all and existing on a lower and non-conscious level. However there can still be intermediate positions, perhaps exemplified by several of the higher animals, young babies and near humans (in evolution), who have flashes of consciousness akin to the striking of individual photons on a screen. In contrast, the flashes of consciousness become a *stream* of consciousness in ordinary man.

There is a further point to the analogy. The intermittency of light illustrates the difference between non-conscious, semi-conscious and fully-conscious beings. But, in addition to the question of intermittency, there is the question of intensity. God is pure light and, in comparison, the human stream of consciousness is like a feeble lantern. Nevertheless, even a glimpse of light is a glimpse of *light*. Thus any glimmer of awareness is, in some measure, an entrance into the divine light and the beginning of an understanding of Mind.

Along with self-consciousness, as a necessary component of it, I believe, comes the phenomenon of freedom, which I shall discuss again in chapter XI. Although one can be more or less free in some senses (for example, in how often one is free and in how strong one is to carry out one's good intentions), in another sense freedom is something you either have, or do not have. In this last sense, stones are not free, nor are rabbits, but men are (except when there is something radically wrong with their brains). As I have said, this does not mean that we are free all the time, but that we have a certain essential capacity which stones and rabbits do not have. It is rather like the case of prime numbers. Either a number is prime or it is not;[17] in this sense there is an either/or, with no third position. But man, I have argued, has this essential capacity so that he stands, with God, on the side of beings that are free, over against the multitude of things in whom this capacity just does not exist because they have not attained this *level* of existence.

As we have seen, the same point can be made with respect to awareness,[18] based on what has been said about God as Mind; about human love[19] as a reflection of God's love; and of man's creative capacity as a reflection of God's creativity (though in the last case what should be said would overlap with the discussion of freedom). In all of these cases, we find that a word can properly be applied to God, at least within a Christian philosophy, because although God is infinitely greater *in degree* with respect to these capacities, he is not totally different *in kind*.

In contrast, many of the other words that we use to describe God are used much more loosely. For example, when we describe God as 'great', we don't mean to describe his size in comparison with ours, but rather we are using a value term by which we praise God. Again, when God is described as 'jealous' in the Old Testament, this is not an accurate description of God; rather it is a roundabout way of saying that there can be no rivals to God. He alone can satisfy man's deepest longings.

Some readers may find this discussion about religious language very academic, but it has important implications. If it were true that human language could say *nothing* that is true about God, then there would be little point in most Christian teaching. Also, the approach that I have outlined indicates an important contrast with many Eastern accounts of religion (some of which will be referred to in chapter XIII). Here there is frequently found the claim that ultimate reality is totally beyond any rational comment or use of human words. We have to rely solely on silence or ecstatic vision. Oddly enough, those who make this claim frequently go on to write long books about God or religious truth! My point here is not to belittle the religions of the East from which I believe that the Christian can learn much, but to insist that it is not necessary for the man of faith to take such a drastic view of the poverty of human language. Provided that we are prepared to emphasize the initiative of God in *revealing* himself, then there is no reason why we cannot say *both* that God is transcendent and that he can be described, though very inadequately, by certain words, in particular 'God is Love' and 'God is Mind', for the reasons we have already explored. We may also be able to say that God is *being*,[20] but this raises issues that go beyond what can be explored in this book.

A final caution should be added about how Christians use the word 'transcendent', meaning 'going beyond' the human dimension. It is misleading to say that God is *totally* transcendent, though this is a phrase one often hears. When this phrase is used as a way of referring to the awesome majesty of God and to our status as creatures, this is perfectly acceptable Christian philosophy. However, when it is taken as an accurate statement about God's nature, it must imply that *nothing* true can be said about God using human words. I have argued that it is *true* to say that God is Love and that God is Mind. Therefore God is transcendent, but not, in the strictest sense, *totally* transcendent.

VII Church and Sacrament

Christ and the church

It often happens that one thing can only be understood properly in terms of its relationship with other things. For example, when we learn a word in a foreign language, we need to know how it relates to other words in that language and to its grammar, before we can use it correctly. This illustrates why I have followed a certain pattern in this book. We began with faith, then the idea of God and then the idea of a creature made in the image of God. After that, we explored the idea of Christ, who acts as a sort of bridge figure between the ideas of God and of man. The remaining chapters do not follow such a neat system, but they are interrelated because one part of Christian teaching needs to be understood in the context of the rest.

This interrelationship is especially true in the case of the church, for we need first to look at the idea and the ideal of the church in the light of the earlier chapters before we turn to a reflection on the very human face of the church as we find it in history.

The crucial context for an understanding of the idea of the church is the meaning of the life and work of Christ. Let us therefore summarize Christian teaching about Christ. He is *the* image of God, incarnate as a man, who opens up to all men a new kind of life. 'In Christ' man can be reconciled with God and his fellow man through a discovery of his true nature. This involves a transformation of his selfish, animal ego, through a death of the selfish individuality which places each man at the centre of his own private stage. Thus the clue to life is a kind of death, in which our very being is united with our brothers and sisters in the family of Christ. This is the communion of saints, the body of Christ, and the new creation 'in Christ'.

Thus the idea of the church is a *community* in which we both lose ourselves and find ourselves, in which love draws us out of our selfishness and in which we become the hands and feet of Christ in the world. Hence the New Testament can speak of Christians as actually sharing in the work of the cross[1] and as being parts of the body of Christ.[2]

The visible and the invisible church

Unfortunately, the Christian comes down with a bump when he turns from the lofty idea of the church in the New Testament to its physical manifestation in the world. We must not be one-sided here, for the human face of the church has its glories: its men and women like Francis of Assisi and the lady Julian of Norwich, its magnificent inspiration to art, its role in social movements such as the anti-slavery campaign and so on. Also, at its best, its worship can evoke a powerful sense of the numinous and can help to bind people together in a caring fellowship. But the negative side is also only too apparent: the pettiness of so much church life, the boredom of much of its preaching and worship when the spirit has gone out of them, the corruption of those in high places, the intolerance and pride of many Christians and so on. Behind all of these negative factors, there is the failure of most Christians simply to live up to their high calling in their daily lives. No wonder that we often hear well-meaning people say, 'I am a Christian but I don't go to church or hold with most of its doctrines.'

I shall argue that, despite the human face of the church, the Christian who has accepted the basic Christian philosophy that has been outlined here ought to seek a Christian fellowship in a practical and physical sense, even though he may not believe all the things that his local community believes, nor approve all the things that it does. However, he must first understand the traditional Christian distinction between the invisible and the visible church.

The invisible church is the true community of believers in Christ. It contains both departed souls and Christians living in the world. It contains members of every human church and, in my view, many others who are not members of any human institutional church. Thus the division between church members and non-church members in the case of the invisible church is drawn by God and cuts right across the boundaries drawn by man in terms of those who are in this or that church. The visible church, on the other hand, consists of the actual churches that can be seen and heard, containing, as in Jesus' parables, both grain and chaff.

The physical institutions of the visible church are both human and divine. They are divine in that they result from the work of Christ; at their best they are sincere attempts to represent Christ on earth, and undoubtedly Christ can and does work in and through them. They are human in the obvious sense that the actual day by day life and thought of each church is left to men, with all their fallibilities and imperfections.

Can it be said that any one of these human institutions is *the* church, in the sense of having a unique authority to represent Christ, with a direct line of command from the Apostles? Here there is great controversy. The Roman Catholic church and many of the more radical Protestant churches claim to be the only true church, although they rarely claim nowadays that only their members can be saved (which was a common claim in less tolerant days). However, they certainly claim that all other Christian bodies are heretical or schismatic and are therefore separated from the main body of the church. Along with many others, the Anglican view, which I represent at this point, is that no one body represents the holy catholic church in a unique way (remembering that the word 'catholic' is the Greek word for 'universal'). Sometimes, *within* a particular nation, one church may properly claim a certain historical priority, as for example the Roman Catholic church in Italy, the Orthodox church in Greece and the Anglican church in England. (We must note here that the term 'Anglican church', or its Latin equivalent *ecclesia Anglicana*, is the ancient name for the church in England long before the time of the Reformation. Historically it is quite incorrect to make Henry VIII its founder. He was one of the instruments in its reform, for good or ill.) But historical claims such as these are only *relative* claims, a way of indicating a particular continuity with the founders of the Christian faith in that country; there need not and should not be an elitist doctrine that places the national church spiritually above the other churches.

The rejection of the claim that there is no *one* church, in the *visible* sense, does not mean that we should not value and treasure the gifts which a particular church has. Imperfect as they are, we may love them for what they have given us and for the traditions that enrich our lives. At the same time, we may be glad that other churches preserve traditions which we can learn from and which can enrich us.

Briefly, there are three rational grounds for the claim that there is no one, true, *visible* church, but rather one, true, *invisible* church.

The first ground is based on an historical argument and is negative in nature, for it indicates that no single church has a substantial historical claim to be *the* church.

The most important part of this argument concerns the claim to primacy by the Roman Catholic church and this is the only part that I shall try to deal with here. This claim cannot be based on antiquity by itself, for the Greek Orthodox church is almost certainly older than the Roman Catholic church by a few years, but this is not the principal issue. The claim is made that Jesus gave authority over the church to Peter in the famous saying 'You are Peter, and on this rock I will build my church.'[3] However, in addition to the problem of interpreting exactly what kind of authority Jesus gave to Peter in these words, there is a grave historical problem with respect to Peter's succession. There is an ancient tradition that Peter went to Rome and died there, which I tend to accept, though it cannot be said to be based on very strong historical evidence. However, it is quite another thing to claim that he was *bishop* of Rome and that he then handed his unique authority to the following bishops. Of course the second century bishops of Rome claimed this, just as bishops and kings down the ages have made dubious historical assertions that suited their claims to authority, but the actual evidence for this claim is thin, especially if it has to bear the whole weight of the case for the primacy of the Roman Catholic church. My own view, and that of many others, is that it is most un-likely that any of the apostles took on the role of bishop within a particular city, except perhaps James in Jerusalem. I might easily be wrong about this, but my point is not that Peter was certainly *not* bishop of Rome, but that there is a genuine ground for *doubt* in this case. And if there is real ground for doubt, then this is a poor founda-tion for the tremendous claims that are made for the unique authority of the Roman see. Let me stress that I do not see this argument as an attack on the Roman Catholic church as such; it is rather an attack on a *particular claim* that is made by it. The historical evidence does not support the view that this, or any other visible institution, is *the* true church. (I should add here that many non-Roman Catholics, including myself, would seriously consider the proposal that the bishop of Rome should become spiritual head of the whole Christian church, provided that among the changes was a shelving of the claim to infallibility.)

The second ground for doubting whether there is one true visible church is probably the strongest. Jesus gave us a sort of acid test for deciding whether or not someone was on the side of God: 'You will know them by their fruits.'[4] In this respect all the major churches stand in much the same light, for each of them is a crazy mixture of saints and villains. Reflection on this test suggests strongly that the one true church can only be the invisible church.

The third ground is based on the kind of authority that man needs. Some Christians argue as follows: 'God cannot have left uncertainty in so vital a matter as who is to be his spokesman on earth, so we must look for that body that now carries his unique authority.' Then the argument goes on to show why this or that institution is *the* church. But there are several flaws in this kind of argument. First, it is ridiculous to suppose that God will only save those who happen to belong to a particular human institution, for salvation is a matter of our spiritual and moral state in the eyes of God. Hence the urgency of making sure that one is, as it were, on the right ship, is misplaced. The urgency is there, but it is to be true and faithful to one's vision of the good, the true and the beautiful. If that leads one into a particular church, that is fair enough, but it is not grounds for consigning the others to hell! Second, the claim that God must have left a unique spokesman runs completely counter to our ordinary experience of how God deals with human problems, when, again and again, he chooses to leave man to work things out for himself. Further, the more we reflect on the nature of man, the more we can see this is the way it must be, for how else can man learn to be responsible, to be his brother's keeper and to become a rational being? Thus we can begin to see why God rarely answers our prayers for specific guidance in a direct way and, in the light of this insight, it would be odd to expect him to give us direct answers to our fundamental questions through the authority of another person. The point is that fundamental answers cannot simply be *given* (as we saw in the teaching methods of Socrates and Jesus); they have to be *discovered* by each person for himself or herself. True knowledge, like true moral goodness, is an *achievement* and cannot be handed out. Finally, the Christian philosophy that has been outlined so far suggests that there is and must be an element of risk in being a Christian. We cannot *know* that our good deeds will be rewarded, we must just do them out of love and, similarly, we cannot *know*, through some specially guaranteed authority, that all our beliefs are true. No doubt there is treasure in the church, but this treasure is in earthen vessels[5] and no man or institution should be put on a high pedestal.

The role of community

The previous section is unfortunately negative in tone, but I think that it is important for the Christian to have the balanced view of the church that I have outlined if he is not to become blindly obedient to it on the one hand, or unreasonably critical of it on the other. We can glory in its gifts and triumphs as a divinely ordained community and, at the same time, we can entertain a healthy scepticism about its holiness as a human institution. However, whereas the previous section ended up on a negative note, I want now to stress the positive aspect of the church from the point of view of the individual Christian.

The aspect of church membership that I want to stress here is our identification with, and acceptance of, our fellow man, which must be analogous to Jesus' identification with, and acceptance of, us. When the non-churchgoer who has a Christian commitment explains why he does not go to community worship, there is often a hint of elitism. 'Look at those in the pews, old so-and-so who I can't stand, Mrs X with her malicious tongue, the Rev. Y with his dreary voice' and so on. Some of these comments may be perfectly apt, but is not the discovery of our humanity an acceptance of such people and a willingness to sit next to them? Further, how realistically have we looked at ourselves if we make such remarks, for is it not odd that the really good do not make this kind of observation? Most of all, the Christian should ask himself where he would be if Jesus had been guided by such sentiments. If he sat down with sinners, is not our elitism put to shame?

There is an interesting difference of emphasis here between the Catholic and Protestant traditions and I am bound to say that I think the Catholic emphasis to be the healthier. In Protestantism, there is a tendency to make the visible church a collection of saved and holy people, marked off from the ordinary man around them. In Catholicism, the stress is on the whole community of the village or town as a worshipping community. The latter stress is likely to touch and influence far more people, but of course it means that within the walls of the church will be a far greater range of commitment and it will be far

65

easier for outsiders to find fault. No doubt there is a middle way here, but I do not want to be in a church community which you can only join when you have proved your spiritual worth. (Indeed, *could* I join such a community?) I would rather be in an embracing church and pay the price of knowing that many of us are poor ambassadors for Christ.

So far I have stressed our duty to identify with a community; equally important is our need of what it can give. Paradoxically, just as it is true in general that in giving we receive, so when we actually participate in a Christian fellowship and give of ourselves to it, we find that we receive far more than we give. As our very nature is social, we need fellowship and that part of the grace of God that can only come in and through fellowship. Who is strong enough on his own and who has the right to believe that he might be strong enough? Someone might reply, 'I am not on my own, Christ is with me and in me.' Perhaps, but does not Christ come to us not only in our loneliness but also in the fellowship of others, as the Acts of the Apostles makes very clear? Therefore, why should we neglect what he offers us within the community, especially in the holy communion (which we shall discuss shortly)? Moreover, if the discovery of our true humanity involves our social nature, in which our selfish ego is transcended, then some aspects of grace *can* only come through a fellowship with which we identify. Once again, he that loses his life shall find it.

Baptism

The claim that some of God's grace is channelled through the church leads directly to the Christian idea of a sacrament. In its most general sense, a sacrament is 'an outward and visible sign of an inward and spiritual grace'[6] and for this reason the world abounds with sacraments. Nature itself is sacramental, for from its beauty many can sense something of its spiritual source. Human society is also full of small sacramental acts, like hand-shaking and kissing, which when used properly are outward signs with inner, and indeed spiritual, meaning. The Christian idea is built upon this aspect of the physical order and claims that, in addition to this general sacramentalism, there are some specific physical acts that have inner and spiritual meaning and power, given us by Christ himself. Different churches have different lists of how many such acts there are and what exactly they mean, but for almost all of them two such acts are central and essentially the same meaning is given to them.

The first is baptism, in which the outward act is either being immersed in water or sprinkled with it. The rite was not invented by the Christians, but they took it over from other religions, together with its universal symbolism of washing and rebirth, and gave it a specifically Christian meaning. Passing through the waters of baptism signified a sort of dying to the old self-centred life and a passing into the new life 'in Christ'. For adults, this act symbolized forgiveness of sins as well as rebirth and when children came to be baptized, which probably happened quite early because of the tendency to treat whole families as units, then this symbolized the child's reception into the Christian family and the forgiveness of original sin.

It follows from what has been said about original sin that this last aspect of baptism must be reinterpreted in our time. As a result, some contemporary Christians want to confine baptism to believing adults (as the Baptists have always done), or at least to those young people who can make a realistic choice and profession of faith. Others maintain that infant baptism still makes sense, even though the baby cannot literally be said to need forgiveness. If a child is genuinely brought up in a Christian family, there is usually no moment of decision at which Christ is chosen, rather there is a gradual learning of the significance of the faith which the child is living within. In the light of this, there is a case for having baptism at birth, for although it cannot signify forgiveness now, it can signify both the entry into the Christian family and the promise of future forgiveness.

It is clear that the subject of infant baptism is one concerning which there is understandable disagreement among Christians, with some approving it, some claiming that it is always a mistake and others saying that it is all right in principle, but inappropriate in our contemporary world where the peer pressure is often stronger than the family pressure. However, there is no need for this disagreement to prevent Christians from working and worshipping together in the same church. Perhaps those churches are richer which tolerate different views and practices on matters that are not essential. Moreover, the basic meaning of baptism is the same for all groups. Outwardly we are washed with water, which symbolizes the gift and power of the Spirit that the Christian receives and the grace that flows within the Christian family.

The holy communion

The second great sacrament that comes directly from Jesus' teaching is the holy communion, often called the mass, or the eucharist, or the Lord's supper. Here, again, Christians did not invent the basic idea of a sacramental meal, but Jesus gave it a new meaning.

Behind all uses of a sacramental meal lies the fact that meals taken together are focal points in family or group life, moments that help to bind people together. A fellowship is both expressed in and strengthened by this corporate act. Many of the Old Testament sacrifices were essentially communal meals in which it was believed that God somehow took part in the fellowship and there are parallels in many other religions.

Finding parallels between Christian rites and those of other religions is sometimes thought to be an embarrassment for the Christian faith, but it should be seen as a strength. Christian philosophy should not be a negative one, but a positive one in which all that is good in ordinary human life is taken up and used with new purpose and meaning. So Jesus took a friendly social meal, that may also have been a passover supper with special significance for the Jews,[7] and gave it added meaning. The occasion when he did this is described in three of the gospels and in St Paul's letters[8] and it is evident that the remembrance of this last supper soon became the central act of Christian worship, as it is for most churches today.

The bread and wine are said to become the body and blood of Christ during the celebration of this sacrament. How is this to be understood? To begin with, we must heed Jesus' warning: 'It is the spirit that gives life, the flesh is of no avail; the words that I have spoken to you are spirit and life.'[9] These words were said, we must note, immediately after some of the disciples were shocked at Jesus' statement that they would have to eat his flesh. Clearly, therefore, we have to look at the symbolic interpretation of flesh and blood and not at their literal meaning. One way of putting this is to speak of the 'real presence' of Christ as symbolized in the body or flesh and the 'life' of Christ as symbolized in the blood. (We may recall that Jews to this day have to drain any animal of blood before it is eaten, because the blood is the sacred symbol of life). Thus, in the context of this meal that recalls the last supper, God uses the outward eating and drinking of the elements of food and drink to draw us together and to share in the life of Christ. He is there, in and through the sacramental act.

It is worth insisting at this point that there is no need for Roman Catholics and other Christians to be divided on this matter, despite the controversy which has raged over 'transubstantiation' (the Roman Catholic doctrine that the bread and wine become in substance the body and blood of Christ). Recent studies have shown how much this old controversy is based on misunderstanding. The thing to remember here is that the definition of the doctrine is in Latin and there has been a tendency to use inappropriate English words in the translation. Thus, while the doctrine asserts that there is a change *in substance*, it also asserts that the 'accidents' of sight, taste, touch, etc., are unchanged. In modern English, it is precisely these things that signify the *physical* nature of something, so that it would be more accurate to say that the bread and wine were *physically* unchanged than to say that they were changed. In any case, recent theological debate between Roman Catholic and Anglican theologians has tended to find that in essence their views were the same and that for both of them the heart of the holy communion is the meaning of the action, in which we receive God's grace and experience communion with Christ and each other.

One other aspect of the holy communion should be touched on here and again the point is to stress Christian unity where there has been conflict. Christians have frequently argued as to whether or not this sacrament is a sacrifice, with many Catholics (Roman and Anglican) claiming that it is a renewal of Christ's sacrifice and Protestants tending to claim that it is only a memorial of a sacrifice made once and for all at calvary. I suggest that Christians should not accept either of these accounts in their simple form, but should say something like what follows, whether they are Catholic or Protestant in emphasis. The work of Christ has a timeless quality. Although Jesus lived an historical life, its meaning is eternal and it has to be taken up and made our own, in whatever time and place we are living. Thus, when we recall the life and death of Christ, in particular at the powerful sacrament of holy communion, we are neither re-enacting, nor simply remembering what was done, but rather we are entering into a reality that transcends our ordinary level of living. Certainly we remember, but in doing so we become caught up in an event that stands for an eternal truth. The sacrifice of Christ is then *present*, in that we can receive grace from it

69

and share in it, but strictly speaking it is not *re*-enacted. Drawn by God's love we offer our gifts (the bread representing our life and work and the wine representing our leisure and our joys) and God accepts them and transforms them, as he does all things that are offered to him. So they become unto us the very presence and life of Christ within us. This is not the whole story of the holy communion, but it is the kernel that can unite all Christians around one table.

VIII Life and Eternal Life

Is immortality important?

The prospect of the afterlife loomed large during many periods of the church's history. For example, fear of hell and the promise of heaven were large factors in medieval sermons and Locke, writing about Christianity at the end of the seventeenth century, described virtue as 'the best bargain' because of the promise of heaven'.[1] More recently, there has been a reaction and many Christians, sensing that this concern with the afterlife was a long-run version of pure selfishness, have gone to the other extreme. Surveys of church opinion have shown the surprising fact that many practising Christians do not believe in personal survival at all except through our family and friends and the influence that we leave behind us. This is a very similar view to that of the Sadducees in the New Testament and most of the writers of the Old Testament.

I have sympathy with this reaction, but I shall argue that it has gone too far. The sympathy is based on a real disquiet at the low idea of God that is implied by hell fire sermons and the egoism of much of man's concern for heaven. Genuine love, as I have stressed, is motive free so far as oneself is concerned. It is only this kind of love that can begin to explain the point of Christ's life and the kind of response that we can give. As a famous hymn puts the matter, 'My God, I love thee; not because I hope for heaven thereby'.[2] The hymn ends with the explanation that we love 'solely because thou art my God, and my most loving king.'

However, a Christian belief in personal immortality need not be based on a selfish desire for oneself, but on two quite proper grounds. The first is the implication of the whole Christian faith and especially of the idea of God for our personal future. If individual souls are precious in the scheme of things, there is something odd in the suggestion that they are simply discarded at death, like worn-out cars. I shall pursue this point later. The second quite proper ground for belief in personal immortality is the Christian doctrine of hope. There is always the danger of this hope sliding off into either selfish desire or wishful thinking, but in itself it is neither of these. We are meant to love and care for our own souls so long as this love does not displace the love of God and fellow man. Moreover, we can perfectly well separate personal immortality that is a *result* of our love from immortality as the *motive* for our love. When the former is the case, then there is a quite proper and joyful expectation of a loving union with God and our friends that death itself cannot destroy. Such a hope is not properly described as a *selfish* hope because the self is not placed above the other and, indeed, the true self is seen to be discovered only in losing our selfishness. Thus there is a Christian hope for ourselves and for those we love that is part of the unblind faith that we seek.

Resurrection versus immortal soul

I am sometimes asked whether I believe in the Christian doctrine of the afterlife, to which I usually reply, 'Which Christian doctrine of the afterlife?' Christians have believed many different doctrines, all of which have been held to be supported by the New Testament. The most important divergence is between the resurrection view, which is strong in Protestant circles, and the immortal soul view, which is found in popular catholicism (the official Roman Catholic doctrine is rather more subtle).

Briefly, the resurrection view argues that there is nothing in our nature that survives of its own right and, therefore, no separable soul that can exist without a body. The word 'soul' refers to an aspect of a living and animated body.[3] Hence the future life does not depend on something that belongs to our nature, but purely on the grace of God who can recreate us, body and soul, by resurrection. This was the belief of the Pharisees over against the older Jewish belief that immortality was only found within the family and the tribe. Moreover, it is often argued that this view is better than the immortal soul doctrine because it places more emphasis on the merciful act of God. On the other hand, the immortal soul view, in its extreme form, holds that the essential self is a pure spirit or soul that can exist without a body.

According to some, a soul of this kind is 'infused' into the foetus at the moment of conception. It survives the destruction of the body and then goes on to whatever state it is worthy of. In itself it is eternal, though it can be destroyed by God.

Both of these views run into great difficulties when subjected to careful analysis. Consider first the resurrection of the body view. What is it that makes the new John the *same* person as the John who had lived before? If we say that it is the same matter that is miraculously brought together again, we face awkward questions. All the time the matter is changing in our bodies and when it comes to the resurrection it is very unlikely that the matter that now comprises us is *identifiable*. The particles that make up our bodies are not like eternal billiard balls with numbers on them; they are more like wave motions or equations, so that it is not clear what it means to say that this is the *same* particle as moved in my body a hundred years ago. Perhaps, then, it is the pattern or structure that make me the person that I am. But if this is the whole story, then the person that was John could, in principle, be recreated a thousand times at once with identical bodies (except for their spatial and temporal coordinates) and which one would be John? This question does not arise within this life because we have a continuity of body, but once this body is destroyed, there seems to be nothing to indicate that this new body really is John, even if the structure of the old John is remade.

Such reflection points towards the claim that, if there is to be a meaningful personal afterlife, the essence of John cannot consist entirely in terms of a physical body, even through its structure, but, for want of a better expression, in some kind of spiritual substance ('substance' meaning not matter, but an existing entity with its own identity). However, this does not necessitate going right over to the immortal soul doctrine in its popular form for this too runs into severe problems. For example, how can such an immortal soul have a beginning or be created? How can such a soul move a body, including its own? (Descartes' problem.) Is such a soul independent of God for its existence? How can such a soul manifest itself or be identified when it is not in a body? And so on . . .

I do not have satisfactory answers to any of these questions and this leads me to the conviction that the Christian doctrine of the future life should be one in which it is held that God has some future for us based on a loving relationship with him, but that what form it takes is something we cannot know. Thus the manner of our future should be an area for Christian agnosticism of the kind already defended. Nevertheless, I shall go on to indicate what I believe is a *possible* doctrine in the light of the difficulties that have been brought forward and which I offer in the form of a tentative proposal for those who feel the need for something more to be said.

I argued in chapter III that as the human level emerges, with the appearance of self-consciousness, freedom, creativity and love, so a new kind of being comes into existence that can be called a spirit (because it is a reflection of God's Spirit). Because it is new in respect to the rest of creation, there is no adequate analogy for it in terms of *things*. We may call it a spiritual substance if we like, but it is not matter, nor can it be described in terms of matter or 'reduced' to it. However, it needs a body of some kind in order to express itself or to be recognized. With the destruction of the body, it is still in existence as a unique spiritual reality, but, without a body, it has no place and can neither act nor express itself, nor be said to live. To live, it has to be given a physical or quasi-physical body (like the resurrection body of Christ). God gives it this body and, therefore, in a sense the doctrine of the resurrection of the body is true, but the body itself is not me, it is rather the clothing that I must have in order to live and in this sense the immortal soul doctrine is true.

Whatever the reader may think of this speculation, it has the following logic. God alone is pure spirit, while matter and the created order as such stand in contrast as the realm of nature. Man, in a way that is unique in our experience (I leave open the possibility of other forms of intelligent and responsible life that we have not met, whether physical in form or angelic), stands somewhere between the principles of spirit and of nature. He is a creature, but he is spirit, or rather he can become spirit as he emerges into personhood and finds union with God. Hence we must be wary of simplistic accounts of man that deny this ambivalence, like modern behaviourism. If we think of a thin sheet of solid ice with liquid water below it and air above, then this may represent the status of man as he lives in a hinterland between the realms of nature and spirit. Man is flesh and he is spirit.

The New Testament ground for hope

The New Testament can be used as a quarry for all sorts of doctrines of the afterlife, such as resurrection at the last day, immediate transference to heaven or hell, or a journey to a place of purgation. I propose to argue that there is only one unambiguous claim in the New Testament concerning the afterlife and that is that God's nature and power are such that the faithful shall continue to live in Christ. But how or when or where we cannot know. The grounds for this unambiguous hope can be found in three contexts.

First, there is Jesus' direct teaching on the subject, brief as it is. He clearly sided with the Pharisees on the subject of some kind of resurrection and to the Sadducees he said 'You know neither the scriptures nor the power of God . . . He is not God of the dead, but of the living.'[4] Thus it is our experience of the nature of God, and of our relationship to him, that is the principal ground for the Christian hope.

Second, there is the resurrection of Jesus. No New Testament passage puts this ground more strongly than St Paul in the fifteenth chapter of I Corinthians, which was probably written some twenty years after the crucifixion. He begins by listing the apostles and other disciples whom he knew had claimed to have witnessed the risen Lord, ending with himself, for he evidently regarded his own experience on the road to Damascus as of a piece with the other resurrection appearances. Then he discusses the Christian hope which he bases firmly on the resurrection of Christ: 'If Christ has not been raised, then our preaching is in vain . . .'[5]

I am not one of those who believe that here there is *proof* of the truth of Christianity, because it is *possible* to give psychological accounts of the primitive Christian experiences that do not depend on a real resurrection and, indeed, this must be so if we are to walk by faith and not by sight. I have also claimed that there has to be an element of risk in Christian commitment and faith. However, there is certainly a solid ground here for the Christian hope that puts it miles apart from blind faith. In the first century, we have evidence of a dedicated group of men and women who claimed to have known the risen Christ and who were willing to die for their faith. It is not unreasonable to say that some astonishing event triggered off this faith.

The third context for the ground of the Christian hope is the experience described as life 'in Christ' which has already been discussed. The point here is that if the accounts of this life are taken seriously then there is already a foretaste of a kind of life that transcends the dimension of time as we know it. This is why Christians tend to talk of *eternal* life, rather than *endless* life (which suggests a going on and on of the same kind of life that we find in nature). The nearest analogy in ordinary living for this new life occurs when we are caught up in a moment of love or beauty and do not notice the passage of time. Similarly, as a person approaches God, he comes to share in his timelessness.

Reincarnation

In the contemporary scene of a growing dialogue between the great religions of the world, it may be helpful to add a note here on a Christian approach to reincarnation, given the importance of this idea in many religions. Another reason is the recent appearance in scientific work of evidence, or at least apparent evidence, for reincarnation, through hypnosis [6] or the testing of children who claim to remember past lives. [7] I am not suggesting that reincarnation has been proved to be true, but that the evidence is interesting and shows that if it is not true we have to admit extraordinary powers of constructive fantasy in the unconscious mind, or the existence of some paranormal [8] way of knowing about the past.

It may come as a surprise to some Christians to learn that many Christians have believed in reincarnation, including Origen and his followers at Alexandria in the third century. So did most of the Cambridge Platonists in seventeenth century England, though they insisted that once one knew Christ there was no need for further earthly lives. The evidence also suggests that many ordinary Christians have believed in the doctrine, despite its rejection by the established churches. [9]

Given the variety of Christian views on the afterlife, I cannot see any incompatibility between reincarnation and the Christian hope, provided that one says, with the Cambridge Platonists, that when one fully knows Christ, the circle of rebirths will end. On the other hand, I certainly do not want to see it made into official teaching. It seems to me that this is another area for reverend agnosticism, wherein some Christians may see reincarnation as a likely possibility and others not, while all hold the same basic Christian hope of a fuller life in Christ.

The last things

We have already come across the Greek word *eschatos*[10] meaning 'last' in the order of time and this is the source of the Christian word 'eschatology' which means the last things, that is, heaven, hell, judgment and the second coming. As with the Christian doctrine of the afterlife, once we leave some basic statement, there is considerable divergence among Christians on these issues. This book is not meant to resolve these issues, but it ought to give some understanding of what they are about and some suggestions as to how they fit into an unblind faith.

Heaven is the *state* of being with God in joy and thereby united with our friends. It follows that it is perfectly reasonable to speak of some people as having a foretaste of heaven in this life. There is a suggestion in Jesus' teaching that there may be many levels of heaven[11] and some Christians have taken this to imply that there can be an eternal progress towards God or into God, which can begin here. Perhaps, at the lower stages, there is the experience of a further physical or quasi-physical period and then, as one moves to new levels, anything comparable with the physical dimension becomes more and more remote. Perhaps some people stay on the lower levels. These, like all other matters of detail, including the possibility of intermediate states like purgatory, should be left to our reverend agnosticism.

Hell is the opposite of heaven, the state of separation from God, which must involve alienation from our fellow men and from one's true self. (We shall see in chapter XIII that Karl Marx has a lot to teach us here.) Some Christians believe that, as part of his identification with man, Jesus experienced at least the *feeling* of separation from God when he cried, 'My God, my God, why hast thou forsaken me?'[12] Thus it is clear that the central idea of hell is a spiritual one and not a physical one. In fact, the preaching of a physical place of everlasting torment has done great damage to the Christian faith for it turns God into a moral monster and distorts the grounds for the Christian response to God. But this does not mean that the idea of hell should be treated lightly. The references to hell in the New Testament are perfectly appropriate provided we remember that suggestions of a physical hell are symbolic. (Apparently many of them are references to the rubbish pit outside Jerusalem and indicate the uselessness of the soul without God, not its eternal punishment.) Whether those in hell will all be reached by the love of God in due time, as the 'universalists' believe, we cannot know also. Those who are attracted to this idea may take comfort in Francis Thomson's poem *The Hound of Heaven*, which suggests that God's love will seek for ever those who are lost.

The idea of judgment is closely related to the ideas of heaven and hell. In former times, most Christians thought in terms of a literal day of judgment in which there were two somewhat contradictory themes. One was an account, as kept by a recording angel, with the good and bad deeds added up to see where we stood. The other, based on the insight that no one is worthy of God's love and that we all depend on his grace and mercy, saw the judgment in terms of whether or not we were 'justified' before God by our acceptance of what Christ had done for us. Many Christians still think in terms of one or both of these ideas when they talk of judgment, but I suggest that there is a third approach to judgment which is more likely to be on the right lines and which borrows something from both of these themes. Our good and bad deeds, and our response to or our rejection of grace in whatever form it is offered, do not lead to an adding up of scores, but to an immediate and, in a way, natural result in terms of what happens to our spirit. (There is some similarity here to the Hindu idea of karma, or a law of spiritual cause and effect, but it is extended to take far more seriously the Christian insight into the reality of grace.) Thus there is no need for a recording angel, because when we respond to the good our spirit grows and we become capable of more joy and more growth. There may not be an immediate reward, but in its own way and time the reward is natural and inevitable, not because we acted *for the sake of* the reward (which would frustrate its attainment), but because we have moved to a higher level of being. Similarly, every refusal of grace and every mean act drag us down. Again there may be no immediate and obvious punishment, but inevitably we have hurt ourselves at the deepest level. We may be able to retrace our steps, but only at the price of the pain of dying to 'the old man'. Thus there is judgment but not the keeping of accounts.

Finally, what should we make of the second coming, that doctrine which is at the centre of the preaching of many radical Protestant churches and which is relegated to a distant and hazy future by the more traditional churches? The principal reason for the uncertainty and disagreement here is that the crucial New Testament passages that refer to the second coming are open to several possible interpretations. For example, in the thirteenth chapter of Mark, was Jesus referring to an historical event after the spread of the gospel, or was he referring to the dramatic meaning of the cross and resurrection that were about to occur, or was he using picture language to describe inner and spiritual events; or were these words never spoken by him but put into his mouth by some in the early church who expected an imminent return of Jesus? It is most unfortunate that many preachers bang the pulpit and declare what the Bible teaches about the second coming, when what they actually give us is *their interpretation* along one of these lines.

I do not want to claim that the doctrine is unimportant, but, as the reader will by now have been led to expect, I think that we should be agnostic about exactly how and when it will be fulfilled. What I believe to be of permanent importance in the doctrine is the note of *urgency* in the Christian gospel that the more traditional churches tend to neglect. It is not that there cannot be another opportunity for us to respond to God for we cannot know whether or not this will be the case; it is that each presentation to us of the good, the true, or the beautiful, in its own way may be a unique opportunity. In particular, the chance to do service for God of a particular kind, or for a particular person, may be gone for ever. Also, there is much to be said for living each day with a sense that it may be our last on earth.

Two of Jesus' parables express this note of urgency with special power. One is the parable of the wedding feast, where some of the bridesmaids are not ready with their lamps when the bridegroom comes: 'Watch therefore, for you know neither the day nor the hour.'[13] The other, which I would closely associate with this in its meaning and which comes later in the same chapter, is the parable of the great assize. At the last day the unrighteous say 'Lord, when did we see thee hungry or thirsty ...' and the Lord replies 'As you did it not to one of the least of these, you did it not to me.'[14]

Perhaps, one day, the heavens will open and we will literally see the return of Jesus in power, but what is certain is that every day and almost every hour Jesus comes to us and challenges us in the way we treat our fellow men and women. If we are faithful in the latter, what need is there to worry about the former?

IX The Essentials and the Non-essentials

Is belief important?

Many Christians have all sorts of particular beliefs that other Christians regard as untrue, or as unimportant even if they are true. Thus, if Christians of many kinds are to share a basic unity, we need to be able to distinguish the essentials of the Christian faith from the non-essentials. The latter can then be an option for those who happen to believe them, or for those churches that want to stress them, but they need not be sources of division.

When we ask what are the essentials of the Christian faith, the first question that arises is whether *any* belief is essential for man's salvation. It seems odd that anyone should be saved or doomed just for believing or not believing that something is the case, that is for belief in the sense of 'belief that'.[1] What people have believed in this sense is enormously influenced by their culture, upbringing and temperament, and to suggest that God would regard such beliefs as essential for a person's permanent salvation seems to make God capricious (rather like the God whom some Calvinists believed in who predestined many souls to hell before he had ever made them). This view has only seemed plausible because preachers have tended to slide over from talking about belief in the sense of 'believing that', to belief in the sense of 'believing in', wherein some kind of commitment and way of life is involved, and then it is quite reasonable to say that a belief might affect our salvation.

I do not want to say that belief, in the sense of 'belief that', is un-important, for if we value the truth it must be important and it is bound to have long-run effects on what kind of people we are. But this kind of belief cannot be *essential* for man's salvation as belief in the sense of 'belief in' might be.

Next, we must note another ambiguity in the question 'What is essential?' This might mean what is essential for one's life and growth as a person, or it might mean essential if a person is to be a Christian, which is not necessarily quite the same thing, as I shall explain. Further, it might mean what is essential for the church if it is to represent Christ's teaching. Again, this is not necessarily the same as what is essential for the individual Christian. For example, it might be essential for the church to have a statement of faith like the Apostles' creed if it is adequately to carry out its teaching function, but it may not be necessary for someone to be in a church with such a creed in order for them to be a Christian.

A three-tier system

The distinctions that I have just made between the different senses in which we can talk of something being *essential* lead me to a suggestion that I believe could go a long way in forwarding Christian unity. It would enable people to see where agreement really mattered, where it mattered less and where it was unimportant. The heart of this suggestion is that we should adopt a three-tier system of belief. Level A is the fundamental one and refers to the belief that is essential for man in the strict sense. It is basically summed up in the first creed 'Jesus is Lord' or 'Christ is Lord'. Level B is what is essential for the church as a whole in order to maintain its nature and to fulfil its charge to spread the good news revealed in Christ. It comprises the basic content of the Apostles' and Nicene creeds. Level C refers to the mass of particular beliefs of individual churches, for example, the belief in the physical assumption of Mary within the Roman Catholic Church. Within a particular church, beliefs in level C may be thought important for the full growth and richness of the church, but there is no need for anyone to argue with other Christians about them as if they were matters of great importance. I also doubt whether any church is wise to insist that all its members must hold to its beliefs at level C, for a Christian might love and respect a particular church, but be driven out of it if he is compelled to swallow his doubts about all of its beliefs.

We shall now look at each of these levels more carefully.

Level A. Christ is Lord

Nowadays, few Christians believe that they alone can be saved, although this was the official teaching of the major churches in former times. From what we have said of the nature of God and man in earlier chapters, it follows that the one *essential* condition for being a person, and therefore in a fundamental sense for being 'saved', is to respond to the good in whatever form it comes, but especially as it confronts us as the morally good, or the true, or the beautiful. The liberal Christian believes that whenever man is confronted in any of these ways, he is in fact being confronted with God. But a genuine response to the good, or the true, or the beautiful does not necessitate that one *knows* that these are reflections of God. Thus the good man of any religion, or of none, can still respond to God. Moreover, when we see that Christ is the incarnation of the *logos*, or word of God, as it comes to all men, we must also see that in a sense such response is response to Christ. So whoever respects the good, the true and the beautiful has begun to treat Christ as Lord.

However, it does not follow that all good men are *really* Christians for to say this tends to make for woolly thinking and confusion. It is one thing to say that a person is responding to the *logos* and is, there-fore, being saved in a fundamental sense and that as a result will more easily come to recognize him whom he has unknowingly served; it is another thing to say that all good men are Christians. In order to avoid confusion, it is better to use the word 'Christian' not simply as another term for 'a good man', but for one who believes *that* Jesus is the Christ *and* who believes *in* him. So the Christian has the joy of stating what he believes to be the truth about God and man and he has the responsi-bility of living out this conviction and sharing it. In other words, what is literally essential for all men is *articulated* by the Christian when he says 'Christ is Lord'.

Here, then, is the solution to the basic confusion over the notion of what is essential. When we ask what is essential for salvation in the strictest sense, the answer is a response to the good, which is however unknowingly a response to God. When we ask what is essential for being a Christian, the answer is to believe and to articulate that 'Christ is Lord' (or the variants, 'Jesus is Lord' or 'Jesus is the Christ', which are essentially the same). We can see this both from the logic of the situation, that is from what follows from the nature of God and of man, and from the history of the church, where we find 'Christ is Lord' to be the first creed. The first Christians were asked to renounce their sins and to assent to this one simple statement of faith.[2]

It should be noted that the adoption of this creed as the first tier or level of Christian belief places people with all sorts of doubts within the Christian fold. To say and mean 'Christ is Lord' is to commit oneself to the way of Jesus in life and prayer[3] and to make him Lord of one's life. All sorts of people with all sorts of doubts are attracted to Jesus because he is seen to represent what is good, or true, or beautiful. All these can make Jesus their Lord and, in doing so, find that they are not alone, but are within a great company that draws its strength from this commitment.

Level B. The church and the creeds

In some ways, it would be nice if this first creed were all the theology that man needed, but although it is all that is essential in the strict sense that I have described, it is not enough for the health of the church nor for many of its members as individuals. The reason for this is that we are, potentially at least, rational animals with minds as well as hearts and it is the whole man that God seeks to draw to himself. Thus the intelligent person must seek a *philosophy* of life in which he tries to understand and interpret God, man and the world, as far as he is able. I do not mean that all who can ought to take philosophy courses at a university, for this may or may not help in the quest, but that in his own reflection and reading each person should try to develop this understanding. This search soon leads to a realization of the limits of our ability to answer many of our fundamental questions, but there is still the demand to stretch our mind to its limits. The alternative is the folly of blind faith or of the equally blind unbelief that is so much in evidence. Blind faith can lead to the horrors mentioned in chapter I.

The church too, as an historical institution, needs a basic Christian philosophy which it can teach its members, otherwise it will not be able to pass on the insights that it has gained into the relationships between God, man and the world. Not every member of the church should be expected to accept every part of this philosophy, because we have seen that the one essential criterion for church membership should be the creed 'Christ is Lord'. However, it may be perfectly reasonable for the church not only to teach more than this as its official teaching, but also only to appoint to teaching positions within it those members who subscribe to its basic philosophy. Hence the distinction between levels A and B. Level B can be taught as official church teaching, but only level A is demanded as a test of church membership.

What should be included in level B? It is partly in reply to this very question that I have written this book, for what is presented here is precisely the sort of teaching that I would advocate as the basic Christian philosophy that is appropriate for level B. Where do the two basic Christian creeds (the Apostles' and the Nicene) fit into level B? In my view, they are both acceptable summaries of this basic Christian philosophy, *provided* that one allows a certain latitude in their interpretation. For example, out of respect for the Orthodox churches, when Western Christians say that the Holy Spirit proceeds 'from the Father *and the Son*', they should be allowed to interpret this as meaning 'from the Father *through* the Son', which is a compromise formula that has been suggested by many. Also, when the creed says 'born of the virgin Mary', some Christians may see this as a reference to a literal and technical virginity, others as an ancient title that is a way of expressing, in mythical form, the spiritual significance of Jesus' birth. Also, the 'descent into hell' has several possible interpretations, such as a reference to Jesus' spiritual agony instead of an actual journey, and the 'resurrection of the body' can also mean different things to different Christians, depending on whether the 'body' is taken in a physical or a spiritual sense. In all these matters, we must be wary of making our interpretation an orthodoxy that is imposed on others. If people can say the creeds with sincerity, using this latitude in interpretation, then let them be counted within the number of those who accept level B.

Inevitably there will always be borderline cases. For example, should John Smith be ordained when his view of the incarnation seems about half-way between the official view and that of the Unitarian church (where it is generally held that Jesus was not essentially different from any other great prophet)? There can be no formula for sorting out such questions beforehand for they are typical examples of questions that demand judgment, or discrimination. The need for such judgment arises not only with religious questions but with many of the ordinary issues that face people in their daily lives, for example, am I being dishonest in leaving something unsaid in this letter to a friend? However, when there is doubt, I suggest that the spirit of charity should lead us to err on the side of comprehensiveness rather than that of exclusiveness. As J. S. Mill said in the context of political and social disagreement, we can all learn and benefit from opinions that are different from our own and hence we should tend to value them rather than shun them.[4]

Level C. Traditions and superstitions

When we approach the more particular beliefs of different churches, there is both a positive and a negative aspect to note. The positive aspect is the colour that a particular tradition can give to a church and without which the world culture would be much poorer. Some of this colour may have little or nothing to do with belief, for example, a particular tradition in cathedral music, but in other cases it may be closely connected with beliefs, for example, in processions and pilgrimages connected with certain saints. An important example of level C is belief in the value of a church order that includes bishops and priests. Personally, I think that there are good grounds for this belief,[5] but I do not want to put it on the same level with the issues that I have been discussing and that is why it would be out of place to defend this kind of church order here. I am concerned in this book with the exposition of level B.

The negative aspect of these particular beliefs is the extent to which they lapse into superstition, or make important what is true but unimportant. In the worst instances, Christians are expected to accept, on sheer authority, beliefs that are downright absurd.

PART TWO

X Evil and Suffering

Why is there a problem?

It is not difficult to see why the existence of evil and suffering presents a problem for many believers, not only in Christianity, but in any religion where God is said to be good and all-powerful. 'Why is there evil in the first place?', it may be asked, meaning by 'evil' the intention to reject the good or to cause harm; and why does God permit the main result of evil, namely suffering? If God is good, he cannot desire evil or suffering and, if he is all-powerful, why does he not prevent them?

The problem was acutely felt in the Old Testament just because the writers were coming to believe in a loving God. This was particularly evident in the authors of Job and of many of the psalms. They asked, why do the righteous so often suffer and the wicked prosper?[1] Several answers were suggested, the most common of which went something like this: 'I myself have seen the ungodly in great power: and flourishing like a green bay tree. I went by, and lo, he was gone.'[2] Unfortunately this pious answer just will not do, at least not by itself. The wicked are not always brought down and, indeed, they often die in their beds of old age, full of riches and honour, while others, including innocent young children, die in concentration camps. Where is God's justice in this?

Some religious people think that the problem can be answered by bringing in the next life. The writer of the psalm just quoted is unlikely to have been thinking of this since the idea of personal immortality only came into Judaism after the return from exile and was not universally accepted doctrine even in the time of Jesus. Nevertheless, many Christians have suggested that the justice of God will be worked out because both the wicked and the righteous will be suitably rewarded in the next life.

However, in conversation with an intelligent agnostic or humanist, I have always felt that this answer to the problem of evil and suffering, at least by itself, was too easy a way out. In the first place, it does not begin to tackle the problem of the existence of evil. Next, it asks the critic to take on trust the existence of the next life. Moreover, the more we stress the role of the next life, the more the critic is likely to say something like this: 'This is a very convenient answer, for it avoids having to see any effects of your loving God in this life. If all justice is to be found in the hereafter, then *whatever* happens here is compatible with God's love. Does not this mean that there is no divine influence or providence in this world?'

In the light of this kind of reaction, the Christian needs to say much more if he is to have an unblind faith.

How far is freedom the answer?

At this point, many Christians will say more by adopting the following argument. God has chosen to make a universe in which there are many kinds of creature, including, as part of its fullness and richness, self-conscious beings who have freedom as an essential part of their nature. Such are men and possibly other kinds of intelligent beings that we have not met. Since it is part of their nature to be free, it must be possible for these creatures to choose something other than the good, for the whole point of their life is that the love whereby they can choose God has to be freely given and therefore has a value of a kind not found elsewhere in the created order. Because of the unique value of this love, a universe in which there are men, with both love and evil, is better than a universe with no men and neither human love nor human evil.

This emphasis on human freedom entails that we must be very careful in the way that we talk of the omnipotence of God. For the man of blind faith, omnipotence often refers to the belief that God can do literally anything, but Christian philosophers have rarely believed in this kind of absolute omnipotence. God cannot, according to them, will a contradiction, for this is meaningless, nor can he will evil as this would be contrary to his nature. God's omnipotence refers instead to the belief that God can do whatever it is *logically possible* for him to do. Thus he can make men who are free, but he cannot *make* these men good; he can only encourage and assist them to be good, otherwise it would not be *their* goodness, but a necessity of temperament imposed upon them by God. We would have nicely behaved robots, but not loving persons. Human goodness, by its very nature, has to be *achieved* not given.

This point is so important for an unblind faith and is the source of so much misunderstanding that we must go into it more deeply, even if the language may seem somewhat technical for some readers.

Let us note that the idea of an absolute omnipotence, meaning an infinite capacity to do anything, is not essentially tied to the idea of God, even when it has developed into the one creator-God of the great monotheistic religions. In ancient Israel, for example, God was the one supreme creative power, but the word 'infinite', in the modern sense, cannot properly be applied for they simply did not have this concept.[3] In the Bible, there is sometimes the suggestion that God can do anything,[4] but this must be understood in the context of a culture that did not distinguish between logical and practical impossibility.

What precisely is this distinction? Something is *logically* impossible when it implies a complete contradiction. Thus a square circle is logically impossible, provided that we use the words 'square' and 'circle' in their ordinary senses. Mathematics gives us many other examples. For example, it is a contradiction to say that the angles of a triangle do not add up to 180 degrees (assuming that we are talking of triangles on a plane surface, for other geometries are logically possible). In contrast, what is *practically* impossible does not in itself involve a contradiction, but is just beyond our powers. For example, it is practically impossible for men to run a mile in ten seconds. Thus 'practical' does not here mean 'almost' as in the popular use of the term 'practically impossible', but 'completely impossible given our powers'.

Now, the important point can be made more clearly. Most Christian philosophers have claimed that just as God cannot make square circles, nor do anything else that is logically impossible, so he cannot *make* men good, because this too would involve a logical contradiction. If he made men good, then they would no longer be men, in the ordinary sense of the word. But this is *not* limitation on God's 'power' as that word should be understood, for when the Bible talks of God's 'almighty' power, this is a reference to the fact that he has the power to do all the things that for us are practically impossible.

The conclusion we reach here is of a piece with many other emphases in this book. While a blind faith frequently makes careless and sweeping claims on behalf of God and of Christianity, an unblind faith often finds that the ancient doctrines contain basic truth, but that they have been misunderstood and put in inappropriate ways. We have found this to be so in the case of original sin and it applies equally to an understanding of omnipotence. Once the true nature of God's power is seen, it follows that, in making a free being such as man, God chose by that very act to accept a limitation on his power. So long as human life involves freedom, then evil and suffering are the price that must be paid for human love and joy.

Natural evil

Although the approach suggested above brings the discussion of evil and suffering to a higher level, it is still insufficient for an unblind faith. An intelligent and friendly critic of the Christian faith might well take up the argument as follows: 'Fair enough, you have shown how evil must be a possibility once man is created and how this evil must be able to lead to suffering, but what about all the suffering that is not caused by human evil, namely that suffering that is sometimes called 'natural evil'? Examples are the consequences of earthquakes, cosmic disasters, animal suffering within the ordinary course of nature and so on? *Some* of this is caused or encouraged by human choice (such as the result of choosing to stay in an earthquake zone after repeated warnings of an imminent disaster, or the failure to spend enough money on cancer research), but much of it is completely independent of any human choice. How can such things be allowed by a loving God?'

This question demands a further reply and Christian philosophers have usually responded along these lines. Any created universe must manifest an *order* if it is not to be chaos and if it is to be a possible context for human life. Events have to fall into a pattern and to be generally predictable, otherwise although we might be able to *will* good or evil for another person, we could not produce actions which were likely to effect this good or evil and eventually it is doubtful whether it would even make sense to will anything at all.

One way in which this necessary order could be produced so that we could predict with some probability the outcome of our actions, would be for God to direct every event, by his sheer will, in such a way that events appeared to fall into regular patterns. However, Aquinas, and most Christian thinkers who have followed him, argues that this is not how God has chosen to make things happen. Instead, he has created something that should be seen as still more marvellous, namely a universe that is *made to make itself*. The created order is then given its own laws, its own causality and its own relative independence or autonomy. Thus nature is not to be seen as a sort of marionette theatre in which the fingers of God directly control every movement, but as an *order*, with a genuine, though not absolute, independence. This enables man to engage in science as he seeks to understand the working of this order and generally to live a human life in which events are predictable.

But if this is the way that God has set up his creation, then God *must* generally respect these laws of the universe and allow physical nature to take its course; otherwise he simply destroys the environment which is necessary for growth. On rare occasions, he might suspend these laws, or operate in terms of higher laws which appear to suspend them, and then the Christian may talk of 'miracles'. However, we have no right to demand that God act in this kind of way whenever it suits us. Suppose, for example, that a thunder storm threatens the life of someone whom we love. God *could* intervene, for it is not logically impossible for him to do so (as it is impossible for him to make our friend good), but if we expect him to intervene on this occasion, then we must equally be prepared to ask him to intervene whenever someone is threatened by a storm, or by anything else in the course of nature. But as soon as we see the results of a consistent use of God's saving power, we find that the necessary context for human growth, in which nature can be relied upon and in which we have to learn responsibility, has been set aside.

It follows that we should be extremely careful when we say 'it is God's will' after some misfortune. There is a sense in which all that happens is *permitted* by God and so some writers have paid lip service to God's omnipotence by saying that his 'will' is always affected, but this totally misleads the ordinary person. When a child is killed in an accident, it is *not* God's *will* in any ordinary sense of the word and great misunderstanding has arisen because so many religious people have talked as if it must really be God's will whenever evil falls. The child's death is probably due to human evil, negligence, or carelessness, in which case it comes under the inevitable consequences of freedom. Sometimes it may come purely from physical and unpreventable causes, in which case it is still not God's will, but the effects of the *order* which the world must have if we are to learn to be responsible and to love.

The role of providence

If we accept the argument of the last two sections, it follows that there is no inconsistency in believing both in a God who is good and powerful and in the existence of both moral and natural evil. One is the result of freedom, the other of the autonomous order that God has to make as an environment for man to live in. However, an unblind faith can take a further step in its understanding of evil and suffering, even though we cannot hope to see the whole picture nor to satisfy every sceptical inquirer.

Let us suppose that our friendly agnostic returns to us with the following comment: 'I can see from what you have said that there might be a loving God in spite of the human and natural evil that we find, but what difference does this God make to our world? If God cannot interfere with human freedom, nor interrupt the autonomy of his order, does this leave any significance to the idea of God? What difference does it make whether there is such a God or not, except perhaps in the next life, and surely you don't want to say that God is only relevant in the hereafter?'

This is an important comment because it reflects the thinking of many intelligent people once they have moved away from the naive idea of a God who alters the world or our fellow men and women in accordance with our requests. In my view, the Christian reply to this comment should be along these lines.

Much of the discussion of evil and suffering has taken place in the context of the assumption that the *end* of life is human happiness. But perhaps a better perspective is this. *The* end or final purpose of human life is both a joy that can only come from union with God and our fellow man and a nobility of character that has an intrinsic value. But both of these depend on our growth as persons to the point where our selfish egoism is replaced by a genuine love of God and of man. Therefore, the primary purpose of this life must be seen in terms of this growth rather than in terms of happiness. This does not mean that happiness is unimportant here and now, let alone that we should neglect the happiness of others, but that it is not *the* end.

If we accept this perspective, then we shall have very different expectations about what we expect God to do in this world and, in particular, how we expect him to answer our prayers. We shall expect God to make a difference and this must be stressed in reply to the comment of the friendly agnostic, otherwise we do indeed make God irrelevant to this life, but the chief expectation is not that God will mould the world as we would have it, but that he will help us to live in the world. He will not so much change the world as change us and then the world through us.

'Providence' is the word usually used for God's government of the world and his active involvement in it and I have written more extensively of its meaning elsewhere.[5] What I have suggested is that it is God's providence deliberately to make a world that makes itself. Thereafter, God may steer it in certain directions, but by use of a kind of persuasion rather than through an overwhelming force. Perhaps on certain occasions he brings about an event by some direct use of his power and then some Christians would talk of 'miracle', but this cannot be the general means of his government if we are to have human character and a context for human growth. God's daily providence, therefore, is active principally through the influence he has on us, analogous to the way in which we influence our friends for good, without manipulating them or forcing their response. Through the good and the true and the beautiful, he draws us every day towards himself and towards our own growth and fulfilment, whether or not we recognize that God is the source of the good and the true and the beautiful. So he is active, but in the only way that is possible given his decision to make creatures who can freely respond to him in a world that must have its own order.

An important illustration of this perspective on the purpose of human life and of the working of providence is the Christian attitude to sickness, old age and death. Within the context of seeing happiness as *the* end of this life, all of these seem pointless, except perhaps for a speedy death in order to make room for other people. Within the context of the view of providence that I have suggested, they can all have a positive significance. It is not that God wills *this* sickness or *this* infirmity or *this* manner of death. The point is rather that God has made a world in which all of these things must occur and when they occur they can be used creatively. Further, given his decision to make man, God *had* to make a world in which these things would occur. The particular occurrence may be evil, because it is the result of some human neglect or hatred, but the permanent risk of such happenings is a necessary part of the human situation. At the same time, each occurrence opens up new possibilities as we respond to God. For one, sickness, old age or approaching death is the signal for a tragic personal decline, for another, any of these can be the signal for a heroic response in which a person comes to terms with the world as it is, accepting what cannot be changed and seeking to change what can be changed (which is normally something within us). If we look around us, we can find many examples of this positive approach to sickness, old age and death, especially in certain old people who have developed a serenity which shows not only that they have learned to accept what cannot be changed, but that paradoxically they have achieved a level of happiness that they did not know in their youth.

In all the reflections made in this chapter I am not suggesting that there are neat answers to every problem raised by the presence of evil and suffering, but that the thoughtful Christian is not simply faced with a blank wall so that he must either give up or blindly accept contradictory statements about God. The more we reflect on the issues, the more we are led to think more deeply about the meaning and purpose of life and as we do this we find that the Christian philosophy of life makes at least as much sense as any other philosophy. Once again, we can be Christians with an unblind faith.

XI The Problem of Freedom

The old and new versions of the problem of freedom

We have seen that the Christian response to the problem of evil and suffering depends in part on the conviction that man is free. But is man free and what does it mean to claim that he is free? The thoughtful Christian who mixes with scientific materialists and Marxists is bound to find another set of questions here for an unblind faith.

It is important to see that the issue of freedom, although an ancient one, has taken on a new form with the rise of modern science. In the ancient world, freedom was frequently challenged on a number of grounds. One was a fatalism that saw a blind fate ruling over every event and this often lay behind the attempt to prophesy in the crystal ball sense. Another view was that the gods played a kind of chess game with mortals; another that astrological powers determined our lives. This last form of determinism is specifically attacked in the New Testament.[1] Yet another view saw one omnipotent God as the controller of every event, human and natural. The basis for this was a concern to guard God's omnipotence, but I have argued that this is a mistaken approach since the view that God has chosen to create a world that has freedom within it is, in fact, the result of a still loftier idea of God.

The contemporary scene is different. Astrology is still a force in some quarters, but its followers usually think in terms of the influence of astrological forces on our characters rather than in terms of detailed predictions about the future, so that whatever we may think of astrology, for most people it is not a radical threat to freedom. However, a certain contemporary approach that is held to be scientific does pose such a threat. This is the view that just as we have come more and more to know the causes of natural events, like rain, so in principle we can come to know the causes of human thought and action. In principle, so it is often argued, all events are totally determined and predictable; the only difference between human thought and action on the one hand and the falling of rain on the other is that the former is so complex that detailed prediction is impossible. But even if detailed prediction is never possible in practice, the very claim that it is possible *in principle*, say to an infinite mind, is a threat to freedom. The underlying suggestion is that we are totally conditioned by our genetic structure plus the stimulations we receive from within our bodies and from the outside environment. Many hold that this view is inevitable once we accept the scientific spirit of our age and reject the superstitions that we allow whenever our private wishes are involved.

The essence of freedom

If we reject the deterministic position and hold to a belief in freedom, as I believe that an unblind faith must,[2] can we say what we mean by freedom?

Negatively, it is quite easy to say what freedom means: it is the claim that although we are *influenced* by the factors of which the determinist speaks, we are not *totally conditioned* by them. There is still an area in which what we call free choice can operate. But we don't have to maintain that we are free all the time, for example, under the pressure of certain drugs, or in intense pain, or during a breakdown in brain chemistry. All that is necessary is that the ordinary human person can make a number of significant choices to select A rather than B. When he does so, he is pressured, but is not determined; influenced, but not totally conditioned.

However, this is only a negative claim, a way of saying that free action is *not* random action, *nor* like the movement of a weighing machine in which the pressure on one side of the scale will inevitably bring it down. But can we also say *positively* what freedom *is*?

The difficulty here is that, outside our experience of human action, we have no experiences of freedom from which we can frame an analogy. In other words, we cannot describe human action in terms of natural or artificial models, like the balance scale, without effectively denying freedom. We are back with the claim made in chapter III, namely that with the arrival of the human level, freedom emerges along with self-consciousness, creativity and love, as a new category. Man is

95

not a complex machine, nor even a complex animal, but a new creation.

It is just here that many determinists miss the point and continue to ask for some model to describe freedom which, if offered, would beg the very question at issue. But there is no conflict with the scientific spirit here. The claim is that there is a new level in human consciousness which sciences like physics and chemistry and even biology are not set up to deal with. Of course our bodies have a physics and a chemistry and a biology, but to insist that this is the whole story of man amounts to a dogmatic assumption of the determinist position.

Three arguments for freedom

It follows from the preceding account of the nature of freedom that no strictly scientific argument can be put forward either to prove or to disprove the reality of freedom.[3] However, it does not follow that there can be no rational defence of freedom, but that (as with arguments about the reality of God) the arguments cannot have compelling force. Rather, they suggest that the idea of freedom helps to make sense of our overall experience and that the denial of freedom leads to at least equal difficulties in our account of human experience. Here are three of the arguments for freedom.

First, a belief in freedom seems to be demanded if we are to be able to make sense of our moral life. We commonly distinguish between actions for which we can blame people and which we call 'voluntary', such as striking someone with intent to injure, and actions for which we do not blame people and which we call 'involuntary', such as falling through a floor and injuring someone below. Without this crucial distinction, it is hard to see how we could use words such as 'ought' and 'should'. The fact that our moral language has developed on the basis of this distinction does not prove absolutely that the distinction is there in reality, but it does permit us to make the plausible claim that human language reflects an insight here that is based on a real distinction.

Further, we should note that it is not enough to say that voluntary action has causes that lie within us, while involuntary action has causes outside us. When we cannot act freely because of a severe mental breakdown, or an inherited brain defect, the cause is essentially within us, but we are still not free. The point is rather that free action is not caused at all in the way that purely natural events are caused. Free actions are influenced by many factors, but the crucial 'cause' is our will.

The second argument concerns the paradoxical position of the determinist. If he is consistent, he has to apply determinism to himself, including his own thought processes. It follows that all the determinist's conclusions, including the one that says that determinism is true, are totally conditioned by the influences that bear upon his thinking. But if he realizes that his belief in determinism is itself determined, then there is something odd about his conviction that it is *true*.

As with the first argument, this is not a strict proof of freedom, or rather in this case a strict disproof of determinism, for the discovery that the determinist has dubious grounds for his belief does not prove that his belief is false. However, the belief in freedom emerges as something more coherent and plausible than the determinist position, for if I believe in freedom, I also believe that I have freely chosen this belief in the light of the evidence. In fact, any claim that a certain position is actually true seems to be predicated on the assumption that we can make a decision about the merits of a truth claim that is not totally predictable and conditioned.

The third argument goes like this. The more we know the causes that go to make us what we are and to influence how we think, the more this very knowledge allows us to transcend conditioned ways of thinking in which our thoughts tend to reflect different pressures that bear upon us. For example, consider the Darwinian theory of evolution. Assuming that it is true that man has evolved more or less along the lines suggested by this theory, then this very knowledge itself produces a new situation. Instead of being controlled by the process, we can now control the process ourselves and, within certain natural limits, we can decide how the human species will evolve from now on. This involves a new freedom for the human species as a whole and I am suggesting that there is also an equivalent freedom for the individual when he knows the physical, psychological, or social pressures that have helped to make him what he is. This is the reason why psychological analysis is sometimes a *liberating* experience.

The point here is very like that of the second argument. It is that *human* knowing and understanding cannot be made sense of without the category of freedom. Far from our thinking being caused in the way that the rain is caused, we think *about* causes and we think *about* the pressures that bear upon us and such reflection is an aspect of that higher level of life which human existence is all about.

The spiritual meaning of freedom

When we begin to explore the problems connected with the Christian faith, it often happens that, after an initial process of weighing the pros and cons of a position, we are driven to look more deeply into the meaning of the faith. This turned out to be true in the case of evil and suffering and it is equally true of freedom. Following a discussion of the dispute between freedom and determinism, we are finding that we need to look at the spiritual meaning of freedom in order to understand more fully what it is.

Part of the fascination of freedom, as it is explored, for example, in great literature, is that whenever it seems almost in our grasp men shrink from it, as if at the last moment they lack the courage to seize what they most prize. Some people have called this phenomenon 'the fear of freedom'.[4] This fear seems to me to be an indication of the spiritual struggle that is the experience of every man as he emerges from the animal to the personal level. This fear can also help us to see why the ancient human virtues are interconnected, for courage is needed to accept the frightening responsibility that freedom brings. At the same time, freedom cannot be enjoyed without temperance, or we become slaves to our animal passions. When we have courage and temperance, wisdom becomes possible as we can make our own judgments and when we judge wisely we become just.

Thus freedom can be seen more clearly to be an integral part of the nature of the mature person, along with self-consciousness, creativity and love. It cannot be described in terms of lower levels of being, but it is one of the preconditions of the truly human level and it is, at the same time, a manifestation of that level.

If freedom is an aspect of the spiritual nature of the person, it would seem to follow that God himself is supremely free and this is puzzling to many people for surely, it might be said, God *cannot* do evil, he must do what is best. What choice then can he have? However, this remark overlooks the significance of creativity. It is no doubt true that God, and perhaps also the perfectly good man, cannot do evil. (They are 'able' to do it in one sense, but 'could not' in another.) But there is still free choice, for there can be many good things to choose between and it is not always the case that one of them must be the best when we are thinking of creative action or creative thought. Consider a great painter in front of a fresh canvas. We can predict that he will produce a great work of art, but not what that work will be. Similarly, it is only in a very restrictive sense that the good man loses the freedom to do evil, because for every evil door that closes to him, two or more good doors open in response to his creative genius. This is what should make the idea of heaven dynamic and exciting, in contrast with the boring portrayals of heaven with which we are often presented. Heaven may include an eternal exploration of the beauties of God's universe and an eternal series of challenges to our creative capacities.

Freedom and grace

As we are led to think more deeply about the meaning of freedom, we must come in time to face the ancient problem of the relationship of freedom to grace, perhaps the most fundamental of all the spiritual questions that concern freedom. The Christian faith appears to claim two contradictory things at the same time: first, that man is free and responsible for his own acts; second, that he depends utterly on the grace of God, that free gift whereby we are first created and then re-deemed or recreated in Christ. Thus St Paul frequently asserts that he would be nothing without Christ, for 'by the grace of God I am what I am';[5] and Christian preachers continually contrast the impossible way sought by the man who tries to reach goodness by his own efforts (like one who tries to lift himself up by his own bootlaces) and the transforming way of the one who finds that he is loved and accepted as he is and that 'while we were yet sinners Christ died for us'.[6]

This seems to be a typical case of where we are asked to hold two truths together in a kind of tension, for both the experience of human freedom and of the unmerited gift of grace seem to reflect profound aspects of the Christian life. But how can we maintain both aspects without adopting a blind faith that accepts stark contradiction?

Here are two suggestions which may help us to see that freedom and grace only appear fundamentally opposed from the narrow perspective that most people have, while from a more adequate perspective they support each other.

First, freedom to choose the good as we see it does not have to in-volve the freedom to reach our full potential in the life of the spirit. Christian teaching has traditionally distinguished between the natural end of man (a full and happy life by earthly standards) and his super-natural end (a transformation of the person through union with God and fellow man that brings eternal life). It has gone on to say that fallen man can achieve neither without grace. But perhaps the natural end is theoretically possible without grace, at least in the sense of the means of grace that are available to man through the work of Christ.[7] I have argued that *it is possible* for man to live without actual sin, even though the odds of any individual doing so may be very small, for otherwise it is hard to make sense of human guilt as a consequence of sin. However, the naturally good man would probably be the first to see that he had the potential for a further end and that for that he needed a relation-ship with God that demanded more than moral goodness. Thus grace would be seen as absolutely necessary for man's spiritual end, but not, in the strictest sense, absolutely necessary for his natural end.

Second, there is something artificial in looking at the problem as if freedom gets us so far and then grace, as it were, lifts us over the next hurdle. It is like the artificiality of seeing perception as simply a subject looking at an object, when, as we have seen, there is rather a subject-object relationship and neither the subject nor the object can exist in isolation. Subject and object in themselves are mere abstractions. Similarly, freedom and grace are not things that can exist outside the context of relationships, but rather are aspects of an encounter between ourselves and God. As we reflect on this encounter, we can emphasize either one side or the other of the relationship. We can look at the sub-jective side and stress the importance of our response and our capacity to be drawn by love. Alternatively, we can stress the 'givenness' of God's grace, equivalent to the 'object' in the act of perception. Strictly speak-ing, however, there is only one experience, just as there is only one act of perception. Thus, just as an adequate account of God's knowledge or God's love meant that we had to speak of Father, Son and Holy Spirit and not confuse them even though God is one, so in our en-counter with God we need to speak of freedom and of grace, without confusing them, even though there is a unity in our experience of God.

It begins to look, therefore, as if the apparent contradiction between freedom and grace results from man's tendency to look at himself as a pure subject, set over against the world of things and of other persons, and from the failure to see that truly human living only arises in relationships with others. Man can, of course, choose to become something approaching a pure subject, but in the end this is to choose death. Only when we give up the ego that we try to cling to can we find real life. Once again we have to learn that it is only through a kind of dying that we can live!

Additional note. Those who continue to be worried by an apparent conflict between free-will and respect for science should bear the following point in mind. Increasingly, scientific method does not depend on absolute and mechanical laws, but on regularities of a general or statistical nature. This is especially true in the human sciences, so that a scientific approach to man does not need to assume that every individual is totally predictable, even in principle. There is a good discussion of this matter in D. D. Raphael, *Moral Philosophy*, Oxford University Press 1981, pp. 91–104.

XII The Bible: History, Myth, or Legend?

Historical religion

Christianity is one of the historical religions. This means that certain events that are claimed to have actually occurred in a definite time and place are important or, in some cases, crucial. Judaism and Islam are also historical religions while Buddhism is not. This is not to downgrade Buddhism, but is simply to highlight a difference in character. In Buddhism, no historical event is crucial, only the teaching. For example, if it could be proved that Guatama, the original Buddha or 'enlightened one', never existed, this would not unduly worry an educated Buddhist, whereas if it could be proved that Jesus had not died on the cross, then Christianity as we know it could not be sustained.[1]

It follows that an unblind Christian faith must have grounds for believing in certain key events in history. Unfortunately, not all Christians agree about exactly what these events are, but almost all would include the life, death and resurrection of Jesus, though the last of these is interpreted in different ways. Thus, the question 'How reliable is the New Testament?' is a vital one for the Christian, for, outside the existence of the church and a number of apocryphal gospels of uncertain date, the New Testament is almost the only evidence for the events in question.

In this chapter, I shall argue that there are reasonable grounds for holding that the New Testament and the most important parts of the Old Testament do have historical value and can support the basic historical claims that the Christian must make. However, it is worth noting that there are some other sources of evidence, few though they may be, and that is why I referred to the New Testament as '*almost* the only evidence'. One of these sources is Pliny the Younger, whose letter to the emperor Trajan, written in or about AD 112, discusses the

Christians in his province who sing hymns to a certain Christ, as to a god. He also appears to refer to the holy communion at which the Christians assembled. At almost the same date, the historian Tacitus wrote in his *Annals* about the persecution of the Christians under Nero in AD 64 and he describes how the sect sprang from a 'Christ' who had been put to death under Pontius Pilate. A few years later, another Roman historian called Suetonius has two references to the Christians, one of which confirms Tacitus' account of the persecution. However, more telling than any of these non-Christian sources, though some-what later, is the evidence provided by a letter that has survived from shortly before AD 200 written by Irenaeus. In this letter, Irenaeus reminisces about his early student days and his personal memory of Polycarp who had died as a martyr in about AD 155 at a great age. Polycarp, he remembers, used to tell stories about 'John, the disciple of the Lord' whom he had known when he was young. We cannot be sure exactly which John is referred to here, but this does constitute personal testimony of a most valuable sort: 'Irenaeus, then, in France shortly before AD 200, was able to recall at only one remove a man who had known Jesus intimately.'[2] To some readers this may seem a pretty remote kind of evidence, but when we consider the smallness and apparent unimportance of Christianity in its first few years, it may seem surprising that any evidence was preserved outside the sacred writings that the church treasured. However, I stress that these extra-biblical sources are not being held up as proofs for the vital historical events; they are rather 'straws in the wind', that is to say, suggestive and intriguing items of evidence that help to support our picture of the early church and thence of the man who founded it.

The fundamentalist debate

I shall argue in *The historical core* that Christians do have reasonable grounds for the central historical claims that they must make, but be-fore this, there are some important matters of clarification to deal with. The first concerns the term 'fundamentalism'. Unfortunately, this word has been used in several ways, but I shall use it to refer to the belief that: (*a*) every word of the Bible is *verbally* inspired by God, so that there can be no possibility of error save through faulty transmis-sion of the original text, or through poor translation; and (*b*) that the Genesis stories concerning Adam and the patriarchs are essentially historical and not mythical accounts. We must note that there is no logical necessity to combine beliefs (*a*) and (*b*), for God might have verbally inspired a series of holy myths, but in practice these two beliefs tend to go together.

The most obvious objection to fundamentalism, which is actually of much less importance than two others that I shall refer to shortly, is that the Bible abounds in apparent contradictions. For example, it is suggested that Jerusalem fell to the Jewish assault on Canaan,[3] but this is then denied in another passage.[4] Again, John appears to make the last supper take place the night before the passover, while the other gospels make it a passover meal. However, for someone who is convinced of the total and infallible accuracy of the Bible, it is not difficult to get round such difficulties; all that is needed is to make one's theory a little complicated, just as the scientist who tries to accommodate awkward evidence with his theory does. Thus one might say that Jerusalem was taken, but then lost again almost immediately, or that two different cities of the same name are referred to and so on. Personally, I am not impressed by such suggestions and see no need to attempt such a defence of the verbal inspiration of the Bible, but this is principally on account of the two major objections to fundamentalism that follow.

The first of these is the moral objection. If fundamentalism is accepted, then it would appear that God commanded the slaughter of thousands of innocent women and children, for example at Jericho and Ai. He would also appear to have struck down Uzzah, most unreasonably, for trying to stop the ark from falling. For the ordinary Christian, these and a host of similar examples are not objections to the Christian faith only, because, as I suggested in chapter II, what we read is not what God said, but what the Hebrews of the day *believed* that God said. What we find in the Bible, especially in the Old Testament, is a growing *development* in the human understanding of God, but this is an attitude which we can only take if we reject fundamentalism.[5] We do not have to reject *inspiration* for there can be many kinds of inspiration, as when men see a vision and then try to express this vision in their own words. What we have to reject is *verbal* inspiration. The words of the Bible, even those of the most original text, are human and open to the errors and limitations of vision that human beings are subject to.

The second major objection arises from a reflection on contemporary experience. It is logically possible that God dealt with the people of biblical times quite differently from the way in which he deals with them now, but there is something very unsatisfactory in such a suggestion for it makes the Bible far less relevant to us. But if man's experience of God in our time is any clue to man's experience of God in the past, then we must accept the fact that when God works through men and women, he does not literally take them over and use them like puppets. Instead of this, we find that God inspires men and women with some vision of the good, the true, or the beautiful, and then leaves it to them to work out what this means and to express their insights in their own words. Moreover, this approach to inspiration is the only one that makes sense in terms of the understanding of man and his relationship to God that I have described, for God seeks to *draw* us by the example and power of his love and Jesus suffered just because God so respects our freedom that he will not, and in a sense cannot, *force* us into his mould. So it is that, in the last hundred years, more and more Christians have reinterpreted their understanding of the inspiration of the scriptures in order to fit in with this understanding of God and man.

There is another major objection to fundamentalism, or at least to that aspect of it which stresses the historical nature of Genesis, which has already been mentioned in the third section of chapter III. This is the necessity of an historical dimension to human character, which makes it contradictory to speak of the instant creation of an adult man or woman. This makes a literal interpretation of Genesis not only improbable, but rationally impossible.

One of the important consequences of the rejection of fundamentalism is that Christians are not obliged to regard all the books of the Bible as being of equal value. Consider, for example, the book of Revelation. This is very likely a second-century document produced during a time of persecution by a Christian who really believed that the world would end soon. The church argued for years about whether it should be included in the Bible and eventually it got in, but it might well have been put in the New Testament apocrypha.[6] My point is not that it is valueless – on the contrary, it contains some magnificent examples of Christian poetry and insight – but I doubt very much whether it should be in the Bible rather than in the apocrypha and it is ridiculous to compare it in authority with the books that were written either by eyewitnesses, or by those who were familiar with eye-witnesses, of the events of Jesus' life. Yet it is on a pathetic and irrational reliance on the verbal inspiration of Revelation that Jehovah's Witnesses and many other fringe sects depend. In arguing with such (usually well-meaning and kindly) people, I deny outright that Revelation has full biblical authority and thereby either shock them, or (as I hope) lead us both on to a creative discussion as to why this or any other book should have authority and of what kind.

Myth, parable, allegory and legend

The rejection of verbal inspiration and of the literal historicity of parts of Genesis suggests that much of the Bible is myth or legend. However, we must be careful how we use such words.

In popular usage, the word 'myth' tends to mean 'untrue', but this is not the strict meaning of the word. A myth is a traditional story in which divine or semi-divine beings take part. Moreover, because it is a a traditional story, not one made up for entertainment, a myth nearly always has great psychological significance. For example, the ancient myth in which Zeus, the chief of the Greek gods, murdered his father, is of enormous importance for our understanding of the psychology of the time (and perhaps of later times). In a straightforward historical sense, myths are neither true nor false for they are not meant to be taken as literal fact, but in another sense they can be true in that they can reveal truly how people felt or thought. In a derivative sense, we still have our myths, such as the American dream or the white man's burden, but nowadays the stories or ideas that are used to express a nation's sense of its role in history rarely involve divine beings.

It follows that to describe the Adam story as a myth should not be seen as downgrading it, but rather as pointing to its symbolic and psychological significance. It might even be called a 'true' myth, in that it presents man as the creature of God and as one whose moral and spiritual problem centres in his desire to make himself the centre of his world.

In contrast to myth, a legend is a traditional story that claims to be about historical people and which is either untrue or much exaggerated; there is often a kernel of historical fact behind legends. For the most part, legends are not of great psychological significance, but some are important, for example, as expressions of the heroic pride of a people.

In the Old Testament, the book of Judges clearly contains much material of this kind, but it is more common to find in the Bible a *mixture* of myth and legend, as in the story of Noah. Here, some great flood (but not one that covered the whole earth!) probably does lie behind the story, but it has been ingeniously worked up into a mythical account of God's dealings with man. As such, the story can have great power and significance for the Christian, but there is absolutely no need to insist on the historical accuracy of the whole tale.

Next, we must distinguish both myth and legend from parable. A parable is a story deliberately made up in order to illustrate a moral or spiritual lesson, whereas myths and legends tend to grow or evolve without the same element of creative imagination. Examples in the Bible are the stories told by Jesus and the story of Job in the Old Testament. There can be an overlap with myth or legend when one of these is worked over and turned into a parable.

Finally, we should clarify the word 'allegory'. This is a myth, a legend, or a parable that is used in a particular way, so that the separate *parts* of the story are given meaning. For example, when Jesus says that the seed that fell among thorns represents the word that is choked by the cares of the world and delight in riches,[7] he is using part of the story to have a specific meaning, while another part has another meaning. In a similar way, St Paul allegorizes the wanderings of Israel in order to explain the experience of the Christian church.[8]

The historical core

A rational evaluation of the Bible brings out the fact that it is an extraordinary mixture of history, myth, legend, parable, allegory and poetry, though all of these forms overlap within the actual text. However, it cannot be stressed too strongly that many thoughtful Christians find this realization a help and not a hindrance to their faith. Although the modern study of the Bible, which treats it from some points of view as it would any other ancient document, sometimes raises awkward and challenging questions, it also brings out the great richness and quality of the Bible and the strength of the basic historical claim that the Christian must make. Moreover, the alternative is a blind faith in the authority of the Bible which is ultimately fragile, for as soon as real doubts or legitimate historical questions are allowed to creep in, one's whole faith is liable to be shattered. This is why some fundamentalists have an 'all or nothing' approach to the Bible (either it *is* the word of God, or it is just an ordinary book), which is the opposite of the rational *discrimination* which we are expected to show in most departments of life.

Let us now turn to the basis of the historical core, meaning by this core the history that is essential for a traditional Christian faith. In the New Testament, this consists of the existence of Jesus as an historical figure, the essential character of his ministry and teaching as recounted in the gospels, his crucifixion and resurrection, and the emergence and spread of the early church. Exactly what is essential in the Old Testament is more arguable, but, tentatively, we might say the flight from Egypt, the forming of a covenant at Sinai, the settlement of the Jews in the promised land and the development of the prophetic tradition with its hope for a Messiah.

Whatever may be our doubts as to the details involved in all of these events, there is an overwhelming case for the truth of this historical core, except perhaps in the case of the resurrection, with which I shall deal separately. If we take the historical evidence for other ancient events, such as the battle of Marathon, there is in fact less evidence for this or for most of those that history books give us as historical facts. This is because when controversy is not raised and no one is thought to have an axe to grind, then the smallness of the hard evidence tends to be forgotten.

In the case of the historical core of the Bible, there are five strands of evidence that I want to mention, though this does not exhaust what could be put forward.

First, there is the need to explain the very existence of Israel and of the church. When we look at the extraordinary history of the Jews, with its incredible continuity despite thousands of years of wanderings and persecutions, there is a very strong case for saying that some dramatic set of group experiences went to forge this people. The events that surround Sinai, even if mixed with myth and legend, are utterly congruous with such a forging. Similarly, the very existence of the early church demands some dramatic set of experiences which could forge the followers of a dead leader into the dynamic body which we find in history. Again, the gospel story is utterly congruous with this.

Second, there is the evidence of the actual documents that have survived. It is probable that the vast majority of the New Testament was written between AD 48 (the earliest of St Paul's surviving letters) and AD 90. We actually have fragments of some of these from early in the second century and the whole text from the third (the Chester Beatty papyri). In terms of ancient documents, this is an amazingly short time between holograph (the original manuscript) and the surviving copies, for manuscripts were continually being copied and recopied and there is often a gap of hundreds of years between the holograph and the earliest copies that scholars can actually handle. Of course this is not proof of the accuracy of the New Testament, but it is an important strand in the argument.

Third, there is the growing awareness of the role of oral tradition in primitive cultures, together with the realization that this tradition could faithfully record the exact or almost exact words of a poem or story over many generations. Modern man, with his reliance on books and machines, tends to forget the role of memory and especially of professional 'rememberers' in the ancient world. In this context, the gap between the witnessing of the events in the New Testament and the writing down of these events in the gospels is a very short time indeed by modern standards (probably from thirty to fifty years). The value of oral tradition is even more important when we try to assess the possible accuracy of parts of the Old Testament, where the stories may have been handed down orally for hundreds of years.

The fourth strand of evidence, similar to the third, is the extent to which many passages in the New Testament are in the form of stories such as the parables, or poetry such as the beatitudes.[9] These are the forms of speech which it is easiest for people to remember with comparative accuracy. Indeed, story and poetry were often used deliberately with this in mind. I tried to show in chapter IV that the parables contain the kernel of Jesus' teaching.

Finally, I would stress the many indications of eyewitness reporting that occur in the gospels. Most interesting of all perhaps are those passages in St Mark's gospel which appear to be critical of the disciples, passages which appear to have been toned down in Matthew and Luke,[10] probably because by the time these gospels came to be written, perhaps around AD 80, the disciples had become heroes. It should also be born in mind that the early church rejected many alternative gospels, some of which can now be found in the New Testament apocrypha, just because they were thought not to be accurate.

For example, they often contained stories of the miracles performed by the infant Jesus which were very attractive to the pious (and still are), but the church realized the difference between what was edifying and pious and what was an authentic and primitive record.

As is so often the case, the force of the argument for the genuineness of the historical core is a cumulative one and depends on putting together many things, including these five strands. One of these things is the question of whether the picture that emerges 'makes sense' in terms of our contemporary experience, for in fact all historians use this criterion, however solid the documental evidence seems to be. An absurd story tends to be disbelieved, however many witnesses and documents are produced. It is at this point that objective and scientific factors in the evaluation, including the five strands that I have mentioned, get mixed up with personal feelings and prejudices. It is not surprising, therefore, that we find disagreement about a subject that raises such emotion as the historical basis for the Christian faith. However, my basic claim in this chapter is that, when all the evidence is put together, there is a stronger case for the historical core with which I am here concerned than with many other historical events that are generally accepted without question.

The resurrection

Up to this point, we have avoided the questions 'Is the resurrection part of the historical core?' and 'Is the resurrection essential for the Christian faith?' The initial problem here is that different Christians adopt three different kinds of position with respect to the resurrection. For some, it signifies a literal, physical event, in which there was both an empty tomb and the flesh-and-blood body of Jesus brought back to life. For a second group, there is an empty tomb and the appearance of the risen Jesus, but what was seen was not his former body, but a new or spiritual body of whose nature we can know little. For this group, the phrase 'physical resurrection' is not really appropriate because it suggests that it was the physical body that was seen, whereas they wish to stress the transformation of the physical body. For a third group, the resurrection consisted of a series of dramatic encounters between the disciples and the presence of Christ. For them, even if Jesus seemed to have a body in some of these encounters, this is unimportant, as is the empty tomb. If the bones of Jesus were found hidden somewhere, these Christians would still not be greatly disturbed because this would not contradict the genuineness of the experience of the presence of Christ, as at Emmaus.

My own position is close to that of position two, but, at the same time, I hold that it is important to adopt an inclusive Christian faith in which the only absolute demand for being a Christian is the creed, 'Jesus is Lord', as I have argued in chapter IX. Therefore I would suggest that the resurrection is related to the historical core as follows. When the resurrection refers to the claim that Jesus is alive and that the Christian can know him either directly or through others, then this is so central for the traditional faith that it is both essential church teaching (that is at level two of the three levels described in chapter IX), and also almost[11] inevitably part of what the individual Christian means when he says 'Jesus is Lord' (that is at level one). Thus far, however, a strictly historical claim is not involved, for personal encounters with the presence of Jesus are not the kind of event which one would usually refer to as 'historical' because they are private[12] rather than public. However, at level two (that is the basic teaching of the churches), I think that the church should go further and make the claim that there was an empty tomb, which is a strictly historical claim, and that the truth is either along the lines of position one or position two above (but leave the option here open). This historical claim cannot have the full evidential support of events like the crucifixion, but I think that there is evidence enough.

What is this evidence? Part of it lies in the very existence of the church, as I have already intimated. Another part lies in the claims made by the disciples, who went around proclaiming that they had seen the risen Lord and dying for their faith. Apart from the gospels, the strongest statement to this effect occurs in the fifteenth chapter of I Corinthians where St Paul, writing in the early AD 50s, lists those who claimed to have seen the Lord, ending with an appearance to some 500 disciples. If these witnesses were all mistaken, then what did happen? Yet another part of the evidence is drawn from the experience of Christians in every age who have claimed in some way to know a living Christ.

I am not suggesting that non-Christian interpretations of these Christian experiences *cannot* be provided, for this would be to overstate the case and to play down the element of *faith*. For example, one can entertain the possibility that there was some kind of group hypnosis, or a complex plot to which many people were party. These would both be examples of non-Christian views of the resurrection. There could also be radical but Christian views that did not see it as an historical event, such as the third position mentioned at the beginning of this section. Thus I think that Christians are mistaken if they claim that the resurrection can be *proved* to have taken place as an historical event, as some books have attempted to show. My point is rather that non-Christian explanations of the events surrounding the foundation of the church are as perplexing and troublesome as the Christian claim. Also, that there are grounds for the Christian claim both in the experience of the first Christians and in the experience of the Christian life as it is lived through in every age. This last point is of great importance, for, as I argued in the case of the five strands of evidence with respect to the whole historical core, the argument must include what 'makes sense' in terms of one's own experience.

Once again, we find that we are dealing with the possibility of an unblind faith. From a strictly historical point of view, the resurrection cannot have as solid a foundation as the crucifixion, but there are grounds for it within history and, for the person of faith, these grounds can take on something approaching certainty if they are matched by a personal experience of the power of the living Christ.

Is the Bible the word of God?

Some Christians will be uneasy about this chapter because I have rejected the doctrine of verbal inspiration and the literal historicity of certain parts of the Bible. However, I have tried to present an overall view of the Bible which sees it both as an historical book that can be studied with an open mind and as a book of unique richness and importance for the Christian. In other words, the Bible *can stand up to* the examination demanded by any critical and educated intelligence and emerge as a challenging and impressive testament to a living faith. Of course, not every reader will arrive at the same conclusions, but the Christian can ask the non-Christian to read the Bible, applying his own standards of critical judgment, and then to ask himself or herself the question that Jesus asked, 'But who do you say that I am?'[13]

Does this or does this not mean that the Bible is the word of God?

The answer must depend on exactly what we mean by the 'word'. In the strictest sense, every Christian must say no, for Jesus himself alone is *the* word. If we mean that the actual words of the original text were dictated by God, then some Christians would say yes, but I have again argued that we should say no. However, if we use the idea of 'word' in the broader sense of the means by which God speaks to people, then not only is the Bible *a* word of God, in an important sense it is *the* word of God, for, so far as the *written* evidence goes, it is *the* Christian source for our knowledge of Jesus, for the events that led up to his life and for the events that immediately followed it. Also, it has an extra-ordinary power to evoke a sense of the wonder of God's creation, of his dealings with man and of the character and challenge of Jesus. For these reasons, I have no doubt that the writers were 'inspired'. So what I have presented is not a negative view of the Bible, but a positive one that at the same time allows for an unblind faith and not the blind acceptance of authority.[14]

Finally, let us note what the Bible, taken as a whole, succeeds in achieving. It presents the reader with the person of Christ. It does this not by simply giving us the story of Jesus, but by putting this story into the context in which the meaning of his life can be seen. This is why we need history and the myths, legends, poetry, parable, prophecy and so on. All of these are part of the tradition in which Jesus spoke and which, together, explain the meaning of his life. Luther put the point perfectly when he said: 'The Bible is the cradle in which Christ is laid.'

XIII Christianity and Other Religions

An approach to the other great religions

Sooner or later, the intelligent person who has been brought up as a Christian is bound to ask: 'Am I a Christian just because of my upbringing? If I had been brought up as a Buddhist would I now be a Buddhist and so on?' Such questions must lead the thoughtful person to wonder whether Christianity really is different from the other great religions of the world and, if it is different, then why one should be accepted rather than another.

In this chapter, although it is quite impossible to do justice to the issues involved, I want to suggest an approach to the subject of world religions which is consistent with an unblind faith and which can also be the basis for each reader's further exploration.

From the start, we have to steer a middle course in this approach, as in so many other things. On the one hand, we must be suspicious of a superficial rejection of other faiths that is not based on a genuine knowledge of them. For example, I once saw a booklet available at the back of a church which gave a one page description of each of the great non-Christian religions followed by a one page refutation of their central views. Finally, it was concluded that Christianity is the only true religion. Such an approach is basically dishonest and insulting to the intelligent Christian as well as non-Christian, for how can one know to be wrong what one has not properly understood?

On the other hand, we have to be equally suspicious of the assumption that all religions are really the same, an assumption which is a very natural reaction to the superficial attempts to prove that one religion is better than another. It *may* be true at a deep level that all the great religions are the same, but we have no right to assume this without a careful study of all the great religions. It could be a legitimate *conclusion* of such a study, but not a premise adopted before we start.

Unfortunately, we all know that a careful study of every great religion is impossible, except perhaps for a few specialists who make this their profession, so what is the ordinary Christian to do? If we are at present Christians, or are attracted to Christianity, I suggest that we adopt the following four-pronged approach.

(1) We describe ourselves as Christians, but avoid saying of any other great religion[1] that it is false, *unless* we are honestly persuaded of this after careful study. In other words, we keep open the possibility that if Christianity is *true*, it does not necessarily mean that another great religion is *false*. Unless we adopt this approach, we cannot be justified in calling ourselves Christians until we have actually carried out our study of the other faiths.

(2) So far as time allows, we should feel obliged to study both our own faith and that of others, so that we can come to understand more fully what we regard as the most crucial questions about life.

(3) We recognize the important distinction between the fundamentals of a faith and the incidental trappings that surround it. For example, if we are exploring the possibility that Hinduism and Christianity are ultimately expounding the same message, we are not concerned with the caste system in India, or the celibacy of the clergy in the Roman Catholic church, both of which are incidental to the main tenets of faith. We are concerned rather with issues such as the idea of God, the meaning of human existence and the way in which man can be reconciled with God and his fellow man.

(4) When we start to explore the core of each faith, we do not only ask 'What is the truth in this matter?', but also 'What is the *emphasis* that is being brought out in this religion?' It is possible that all the great religions are saying the same thing at a very deep level and that they are all responses to the same spiritual reality, but at the same time that they are significantly different in what they emphasize. I shall pursue this point in the next section.

Differences of emphasis

In the following sections, I am going to make brief comments on four of the major alternatives to Christianity: Buddhism, Hinduism, Islam and the Bahai faith. It is important that the purpose of each of these sections be understood, for they are not meant to be attempts to prove that these religions are false, because, as I have argued, it is not essential for Christians to believe that they are false and if they can be shown to be false this can only be after lengthy study. However, there is no doubt that these religions do have different emphases, not just at the superficial level that I have described as the trappings of a religion, but at a more significant level. I am still leaving open the possibility that at the deepest level of all these differences of emphasis may be unimportant, so what I am referring to in this discussion of the emphasis of each faith is a sort of intermediate level.

Thus, in each of the following sections, I propose to indicate one or more differences of emphasis between Christianity and another religion. This should help the reader to see what Christianity stands for and where, at this level, there are real differences between the world religions that we must take account of. Then, in those cases where I think it possible to see where a creative dialogue might begin between Christians and members of another faith, I shall suggest how the difference might disappear at a deeper level of discussion.

Before listing these emphases that one finds in the great non-Christian religions, the chief emphasis of the Christian faith should be underlined. One is tempted to say that this is love and in a fundamental way this is true, but since so many of the other great religions also stress the importance of love or compassion, it is misleading to put this down as the chief *distinctive* difference of emphasis, even if the Christian believes, as I do, that the Christian faith has something to say about love that is not easily found in other faiths. Therefore, the emphasis that I would stress is the idea of the incarnation, whereby the Christian holds that God identified himself with man, in the manner explored in chapters IV to VI. Many other religions speak of the 'incarnations' of God, but they tend to mean that God can be seen in the inner core of a truly good man because, in a sense, this inner core is divine. This is one of the cases where we have to be very careful about our use of words for here we can easily be led into thinking that there is no significant difference because the same word is used for different ideas. While the Christian does not deny that we can see something of God in the soul of every good man, when he speaks of the 'incarnation' of God in Jesus, he means something much more than this. He means that the creative source of the universe, who is ultimately *other* than his creatures although he can be united with them, chose to identify himself with man in an act that, so far as we know, is unique.[2] Jesus not only reveals God because of his goodness, he reveals the *initiative* of God because he is the express image of God, united with man so far as it is possible for the eternal to be so united.

As a result of this emphasis, many Christians say that although other great religions are not false and indeed may be true in what they teach as fundamental, they are nevertheless *incomplete* in comparison with Christianity because they do not teach that God's love led to an incarnation, in the specifically Christian sense of 'incarnation'; nor do they teach the trinitarian conception of God, which Christians may hold to be a logical consequence, both of the claim that God is 'Love' or 'Mind' (as we saw in chapter VI) and of this view of the incarnation. Whether this is the best attitude for the Christian to have towards the other faiths I leave readers to decide for themselves.

Buddhism

The aspect of Buddhism that I want to single out is the response of the individual to suffering. Central to Buddhist thought is the claim that suffering is caused by desire and, therefore, that the way to remove suffering is to remove desire. From this comes the familiar picture of the Buddhist saint who acquires complete tranquillity by finding *detachment*. The goal here is very similar to that of the great Stoics, who held that while in one's actions one must do everything in one's power to alleviate suffering, in one's inner heart and mind one must be unmoved and detached both from the sufferings of others and of oneself. For example, the great Stoic Epictetus said that when you see someone suffer you must be prepared to groan with him, in order to help him, but one must not groan in one's inner being, only outwardly: 'Sigh, but do not sigh with the heart.'[3]

Thus there is a startling contrast between the tranquil and detached Buddhist or Stoic and Jesus on the cross, where the demand to love involves *both* outward action and inner suffering. This is not morbid and useless, first, because in many instances only this kind of identification seems really to help, and second, because not only are endless vistas of suffering opened up (so long as there is suffering among men), but there are also endless vistas of joy opened up, which can only come with fellow-*feeling*. Thus the Christian is told: 'Rejoice with those who rejoice, weep with those who weep.'[4]

So it appears that the Christian ideal of love involves a demand to be *attached* in a way that both exposes us to suffering and opens up a new joy in the communion of saints. Also, we are called to have an identification with all mankind that can mirror in its own small way Christ's identification at Bethlehem.

This can be put in another way. We are sometimes told that the command to love our neighbour is not a command to *like* him, because this may be impossible, but a command to the will to act for his best interests. I think that this is misleading and indicates an easy way out of the hard challenge made to us by Christ's command; it also helps to explain much of the callousness of some periods of Christian history. The New Testament picture of love is one of both doing and of caring in one's heart. Of course we cannot, by a mere act of will, immediately feel for our neighbour and this is what gives plausibility to the cold doctrine just expressed. But we can begin to love in the full sense by taking the steps which we pray will lead to a complete love through the work of the Holy Spirit. For example, we are told not only to *act* with charity, but to pray for others in a way that will open up our hearts to feeling. Jesus not only *acted* with kindness towards sinners, he had *compassion* for them and he commanded us to love with heart and soul and mind and strength.[5]

It follows that at this intermediate level there is an important contrast between the Christian ideal of love, symbolized and climaxed in the cross, and the Buddhist ideal of detachment. How then can I suggest that at the deepest level this distinction may seem superficial? The answer I suggest goes like this. We have assumed too easily that we know what the Buddhist means by 'desire'. The Buddhist also speaks of compassion and of a search for blessedness, so that perhaps we tend to misunderstand each other through the words that we use to translate subtle ideas. For the Christian, there is a right desire and a wrong desire, the latter connected with the fulfilment of the selfish ego. If Christians and Buddhists could sit down and explore together the kind of desires that we ought to have and those that we ought not to have, then perhaps it might turn out that many or all of the differences vanish. Meanwhile, I suggest that the presence of Buddhism should challenge Christians to think more deeply about the kind of love and compassion that they should have for their fellow men, for themselves and for animals.

Hinduism

The aspect of Hinduism that I want to single out is the claim that when our souls have finished their journeys and have become perfect, they are joined with the great soul, or that ultimate reality which they call Brahmin, on the analogy of a drop of water being reabsorbed into the ocean from which it came. For Hindus who belong to the Advaita Vedanta school of Hinduism,[6] this means that our present individuality is a sort of transient illusion and that when we truly find ourselves, there is a losing of ourselves into the great 'One'.

On the surface this looks very similar to many things in Christianity, for Jesus taught that we must lose our life in order to find it, that he and the Father are one and that the kingdom of God is within. However, most Christians have interpreted these sayings in a way that is different from Hindu doctrine, as we have seen during our brief discussion of Christian mysticism.[7] The Christian would tend to say something like this. As we die to the old self, a new kind of unity with others and with God becomes possible; but this unity is not an *identity*, it is rather something symbolized in the union of two lovers in which there is still an I and a Thou. Thus, in the incredible richness of God's creation, there is believed to be a continuing place for the person that is you and the person that is I, though both must be transformed.

Here too, while there is a striking contrast of emphasis between the goal of the soul in Christianity and in Vedantic Hinduism, once again we can begin to see the lines along which a deeper study might find common ground. We keep using words like 'self' and 'unity' with only a dim understanding of their full meaning and with inadequate analogies. Therefore, in the presence of Hinduism, the Christian is challenged to think more deeply about the nature of man and of that unity which we should all seek.

Islam

There are two aspects of Islam which I want to single out. The first is the fatalism of popular Islam which is based on an overwhelming emphasis on the transcendence of God and on his sovereign will as the source of all that happens. Thus, when a child is killed in an accident, or there is any similar disaster, the immediate response is 'It is the will of God.' Many Christians have tended to say this too and I have argued[8] that this is a grave mistake based upon a faulty analysis of God's omnipotence. In choosing to make a world, and even more in choosing to make mankind, God also chose to limit himself.

Thus there is certainly a contrast between the absolute rule of God in popular Islam and the kind of Christian view of God's omnipotence that I have defended (and which would be supported by many Christian philosophers, both Catholic and Protestant). But I do *not* present this as an attack on Islam as such, only, as I have hinted, at *popular* Islam, which naturally enough shares many of the crude and simplistic ideas of God that can be found in popular Christianity. In other words, I do not believe that this fatalism is essential to Islam.

The second aspect is the claim that Muhammad is the *last* of the prophets. This is a different kind of claim from that made by Christians concerning Jesus, for Christians say that Jesus was more than a prophet, as we saw in the earlier discussion of the meaning of 'incarnation'. Prophets, in the traditional view, came as messengers of God with a message for the time. Thus, to insist that anyone is the last of these seems to many to be a strange claim. Is it the case, for example, that Muhammad's message, great as it was, was more important for mankind than that of Francis of Assisi, with his vision of the place of animals and physical nature in the religious understanding of creation? Why then is it necessary to insist that the great line of prophets ends with Muhammad?

Once again, I can see what may be a way through to a deeper appreciation of the emphasis of another faith in which apparent disagreements become resolved. In this case, we need to explore more carefully what we mean by a 'prophet' and the difference between someone who speaks within a particular tradition, like Francis, and someone who has to begin a new tradition in order for his message to be effective.

The Bahai faith

We could continue with a discussion of several more great religions of the world, but I shall deal with only one more here, indicating three aspects of the Bahai faith that invite comment. The first is the emphasis on *continuing revelation*, which is a central theme in the religion founded by Baha'u'llah (1817–1892). This is almost an opposite emphasis to that of a *last* prophet! On this theme, the Christian need find no conflict, only he would tend to describe the continuity of revelation rather differently than Bahais. The Christian would speak of continually uncovering what is implicit in the work and words of Christ, whereas the Bahai tends to speak of the disclosure of new truth. There is no need for fundamental disagreement here.

More difficult and controversial is the claim that Baha'u'llah is *the* prophet of his time (apart from his forerunner known as the *Bab*), whose message demands a new religion and who will not be succeeded by another great prophet for at least one thousand years. Much as I respect Baha'u'llah, it is not obvious that he is *greater* than some of the other great spiritual figures of the nineteenth century such as his contemporary, the great Japanese woman prophet Nakayama Miki, founder of the religion known as Tenrikyo. This was at first a religion confined to Japan, but is rapidly becoming a world religion with a special emphasis on healing. (There are also some great twentieth-century figures, such as Morihei Ueshiba, founder of Aikido, who may well turn out to be as spiritually significant as Baha'u'llah. To point this out is not to attack the Bahai faith so much as to question a particular claim that Bahais usually make.)

A third aspect of the Bahai faith is the stress on the need for a world community and here there can be almost universal agreement among the followers of the great religions of the world.

Marxism

Some readers may be surprised to find a section on Marxism within a chapter on the great religions of the world, but even if we are not happy about referring to Marxism as a religion, it is similar to religion in many ways. In particular, we can see how it demands and receives a loyalty from many of its followers which is extremely like religious faith. There is a doctrine, often taught with all the enthusiasm and dogmatism with which Christianity used to be taught to whole nations in the Middle Ages. There are 'holy' books such as the Communist Manifesto and Chairman Mao's red book, which are given a special status and authority. There are 'holy' places, like Lenin's tomb, and a host of other parallels to religion as it is commonly found. Most important of all, in many parts of the world it is a rival to Christianity, or to the other great spiritual religions, for the hearts and minds of mankind. It is appropriate, therefore, that it should be considered here.

I propose to mention two of the basic problems in Marxism, both of which have led many Christians to the view that Christianity offers a more coherent philosophy of life than does Marxism. Then I shall indicate how, despite these problems, Marxism has something positive to say to Christians. However, I must make clear that in this section I am going to discuss Marxism rather than the views of Marx himself, which sometimes differed considerably from the later interpretations of his thought. For example, it was Lenin, not Marx, who propounded the view that a small party, who thought that they *knew* what was truly good for man, had the right and duty to take power by force, whatever the wishes of the majority. Again, it was Lenin who stressed that all aspects of traditional morality were secondary to the over-riding moral command to hasten the revolution of the proletariat.

In a fuller discussion of Marxism, I would concentrate on the Marxist theories of materialism and of economic determinism and the way in which these neglect the spiritual side of man as this can be found in human experience. Here, however, I am concentrating on two specific problems. The first is the Marxist claim that Marx and Engels had done for history and economics what Darwin had done for biology, that is, discovered *the* science of history and economics.[9] The hallmark of scientific knowledge is that the truth of the claims is virtually forced on all rational minds who study the evidence and the argument. However, large numbers of brilliant historians and economists are not convinced by Marx's writings and it is absurd to suggest that they are all simply stupid. In other words, the claim to have discovered *the true science* in these fields is thoroughly dogmatic and 'unscientific'. Christians, as we have seen, do not normally claim to *know*, but rather to believe, although they claim some rational grounds for their faith. The result is that, somewhat paradoxically in view of what is often said, Christianity is much less dogmatic than Marxism.

The second major problem is the claim that human materialism, meaning our selfish and unsocial drives, is essentially environmental. This is necessary for the Marxist belief in the possibility of a classless society in which there will be no state and no coercive law, but in which all will work willingly for the common good. The Christian view is that, although much of our selfishness may be environmental, much of it also flows from our nature, as we saw when discussing the notion of original sin, a doctrine which, although it needs restating, seems to contain a profound truth. It may be possible for a particular individual to grow up without any selfishness, but for a whole society to grow up in this way seems to most Christians to be based on a naive view of human nature. The picture that I have drawn of man as a being who must struggle with his animal nature in order to emerge into the spiritual or personal realm seems to me to be far more coherent than the Marxist view and far more in line with the evidence that we have.

On the other side of the story, there are three positive aspects of Marxism that have led some Christians to see Marx as a sort of misguided Christian prophet! First, there is his stress on the economic aspects of human life, especially those relating to our work. Even though we may be spiritual beings, at least potentially, we have to manifest our spiritual nature in our everyday life, and this includes the economic and social system of which we are part. Christians, and others, have paid too little attention to the implications of this. Second, and closely related to the first point, is Marx's teaching on alienation. It is an 'alienation' from the work of our hands, forced upon many people because of the context in which they work, which tends to alienate us from our fellow man, from nature and even from ourselves. What Marx has to say here is of profound importance, for what 'alienation' means to him has many similarities to what 'sin' means to the Christian. In other words, much of what Marx has to say of human alienation can enrich the Christian understanding of sin and of the sources of sin. Third, and related to both of the above points, is the need for a critical appraisal of our social and political system. It is not that the Christian message can be translated into a purely social gospel, for this is to be blind to other vital aspects of the gospel as they relate to our understanding of God and of man. However, our social and political systems have such enormous effects on the lives of ordinary people and influence their freedom and opportunities for development so intimately that they cannot be ignored. In my own view the required critical approach does not entail anything like the introduction of communism (partly because of the deplorable results in terms of human freedom of all such sweeping changes that we can observe), but it does suggest the possibility of some radical changes in Western democracy.

XIV The Rational Defence of the Christian Faith

Three sorts of argument

The principal aim of this book is to expound the essentials of the Christian faith and, therefore, to say what it is rather than to show that it is true. However, it is impossible to draw a sharp line between describing what Christians believe and why they believe, so that on several occasions I have had to examine the grounds for Christian faith, for example, in the discussion of the resurrection and of the reliability of scripture. In this chapter, we shall look more directly at the problem of how faith can and should be supported by reason.

When someone argues in defence of a faith, there are three kinds of argument that are relevant. First, there are what I shall call 'positive arguments', in which one seeks to show that a certain belief is true, or at least plausible, from arguments that appeal to the general experience of man rather than to private and personal experience. I shall briefly outline four of these positive arguments in the next four sections. These are not presented as 'proofs' for reasons discussed in the first chapter, but they are offered as providing reasonable grounds for belief in God. None of these four arguments is specifically Christian and they can be used equally by Muslims and other theists. Positive arguments for a more specifically Christian faith have been suggested in chapters IV to VI and during the discussion of the resurrection in chapter XII.

Second, there are what I shall refer to as 'negative arguments'. Here one tries to show that alternative philosophies of life are false or inadequate. There have already been some examples of this kind of argument, for example in the discussions of Marxism and of determinism, and in pp. 129–130 I shall briefly consider modern secular humanism.

Third, there is the kind of argument that can be drawn from personal experience, either in the form of events in one's own life that one believes to be providential or miraculous, or in the form of inner feelings of joy or of strength that seem to indicate a direct encounter with God. It is hard to base arguments on such events or feelings that are likely to convince others, but these things may form a powerful argument for the one who experiences them. I shall briefly consider some of these experiences in the last section.

Creation as an act of will

Since mankind first began to wonder, he has asked himself how there came to be a world or a universe at all. Some have put the question this way: 'Why is there something rather than nothing?' To feel the force of this question, we need to share in the sense of amazement and awe that many people feel when they see the heavens in their glory on a cloudless night, or when in other contexts we are overwhelmed by the beauty and wonder of nature. If anything, modern science has sharpened the question, partly by adding to our knowledge of the immense richness of nature and partly by the gathering evidence that the whole universe started with a collosal cosmic explosion some fifteen to twenty billion years ago.

In the past, many thinkers have claimed that the very existence of the universe proved that there must be a creative source that is itself outside the spatial and temporal limits of the universe, namely God. More modestly, I suggest that, although it cannot be *proved* that the universe has such a source, the universe suggests a creator and only if it is the result of the will of such a creator can any sort of *explanation* be offered for the universe. (This is not a proof because while it is always reasonable to ask questions about the origin of things within the universe, we cannot prove that it is reasonable to ask questions about the origin of the universe as a whole.)

This argument that there must be a source of the universe is sometimes countered as follows: 'If you make God the author of the universe and the being who explains its existence, then you simply put the question of why anything exists one step further back, for who made God, or what is the explanation for his existence?' This counter-attack is understandable, but it is based on a mistake. There is nothing in the nature of matter, or of light, or of any other constituent of the physical universe to suggest that it is eternal. Therefore the question 'Where does it come from?' seems to many people a perfectly reasonable question. But the very idea of God is of a being who transcends space and time, so that questions such as who made him, or what accounts for his existence, can have no sense. They merely indicate that the questioner has not understood the idea of God.

Order and beauty as the work of Mind

Among the traditional arguments for the existence of God, the argument from design is the most popular. This argument is based not on the existence of the universe as such, but on the order and beauty that it displays. Instead of asking, 'Why is there something rather than nothing?', this argument starts with the question, 'How is it that nature displays an order that is not only beautiful, but that is so well fitted for the emergence and support of human life?' The force of this question is felt through the same kind of amazement that was referred to in the last section, only with the emphasis on the wonder of each detail and the wonder of the order and harmony of the whole.[1]

As with the first argument, it is important not to overstate it. For example, it cannot provide *proof* for the existence of a designing Mind behind the universe, because it is always possible to insist that what we call the beauty of nature is merely a reflection of the way that we are conditioned to see it and that the perfect fitness of the environment for human life can be explained, at least partially, by Darwinian theories. The environment has conditioned what can survive, so of course anything that lives has to fit into the order of nature.

The last point indicates that the way in which the argument from design is put depends a great deal on one's attitude to modern science. In the old days, Christians tended to see the handiwork of God in the *gaps* which science could not explain,[2] but more and more Christians are tending to see this as a mistake. The superficial reason for seeing this as a mistake is the embarrassment felt as science seems to fill in more and more of the gaps, thus leaving the idea of God unnecessary for those who saw God's role in this way. The proper reason for seeing the gap theory as a mistake is that God works typically *in and through* natural processes. From this point of view, neither science in general nor Darwinism in particular pose a threat to the Christian interpretation of the universe. God has chosen to make a universe that makes itself and evolution is yet one more example of the marvellous system that he has created.

As with the first argument, once the claim to a strict proof is abandoned, the argument from design can be, in its own way, a powerful and legitimate form of argument. The more we see the wonder and richness of nature, the more the Christian feels that the universe suggests or points to the Mind that lies behind it.

The moral order grounded in God

It is easy to see how, during the evolution of human society, there developed certain taboos and other social restrictions on human action in order to preserve society. For example, unless a particular group had some rules about the use of violence within that group, it would not survive, especially if it were competing with a rival group for a scarce supply of food. However, there is a gulf, which it is very difficult to explain, between the taboos and customs which are necessary for group survival and the developed moral law as it is felt by most men and women. It may be true that this law is more often honoured in the breach than in the observance, as the saying goes, but the point is not how well the moral law is kept, but the fact that it is felt to be there as an ideal which we *ought* to obey.

Attempts to reduce this moral law to the demands of group survival run into many difficulties, for men often face a moral demand which puts their own survival and sometimes even that of their group at risk. One can even imagine cases where men might feel a moral duty to risk the whole human species, for example, if our survival as a human race depended on the pollution of the galaxy and the consequent death of many life forms, some of which might be as intelligent and sensitive as ourselves. Even the possibility of this calls in question the view that morality is only a reflection of group survival. In general, the experience of human love suggests the discovery of a dimension of being that goes beyond the rules for the survival of any species.

Once again, the argument must not be overstated. It is not that a non-religious explanation of morality is simply impossible, especially since we cannot predict in advance what future suggestions may be made. The argument is rather that the sense of *ought* which mankind experiences and the nature of the call to *love* one another are utterly congruous with and suggestive of man's spiritual nature. If man is a child of God and a creature who is emerging from the animal level to the personal or spiritual level, then the moral dimension can be understood as one aspect of this higher level (along with self-consciousness, freedom and creativity, which are all inseparably linked with the capacity to love). Seen in this way, it is no longer surprising that the moral dimension transcends the requirements of survival, for the spiritual life must go beyond the egoism of the animal life, however innocent this may be.

It follows that morality, and especially our awareness of love, point to a source of this love that is itself outside of man, a source which both plants the seed, or potentiality, for the capacity to love within human nature and which then draws out this potentiality by the power and example of love. Only in this way can any *explanation* be offered for the extraordinary phenomenon of love.

We must note, however, that when the Christian suggests that the moral dimension is grounded in God, he does not mean that morality is simply a matter of what God wills.[3] The position is much more interesting than that. God is, in his very nature, the Good, the True and the Beautiful. What he wills is always good, because he wills in accordance with his nature, but it is not his sheer willing that makes something good. It is rather that God's loving nature is the source of all good and his will must always reflect this.

The common elements in religious experience

The sympathetic study of different world religions has brought into focus the important fact that the great religions share certain fundamental types of experience, for example, the sense of the numinous, the experience of inner power and grace, the sense of union with the divine and a sense of universal compassion. Even if, as individuals, we never have any of these extraordinary experiences, we can be aware that they occur and aware of the universality of their occurrence. Thus, the argument which I am building up here is not an argument from private experience of the kind to be discussed in the last section, but a *general* argument based on types of experience that are common to many people. Hence, it is a 'positive argument', analogous to others that appeal to evidence that is open to all who care to examine it. The argument itself consists of the suggestion that the universality of these experiences points to a spiritual reality which is encountered by certain men and women in all religions.

Once again, the argument must not be overstated, as if there were a strict *proof* here for the truth of religion. In the first place, different religions often interpret these experiences somewhat differently and, more importantly, there is always the possibility of non-religious interpretations of all religious experience.[4] From one point of view, all religious experiences are also psychological experiences and all sorts of psychological interpretations have been put forward, such as those of Freud.[5] The Christian should in no way deny that psychology can study these experiences and illuminate them, but he may wonder whether *purely* psychological explanations can ever be adequate. Certainly Freud's suggestions seem naive and inadequate.[6] At this point, the 'positive argument', based on the suggestion that the religious experience of man points towards a spiritual reality, begins to overlap with the 'negative argument' that other interpretations of experience are inadequate.

A final point should be made in respect of this argument. When our knowledge of the religious experience of others is coupled with the observation of outstanding sanctity, as in the case of Francis of Assisi, then the suggestion that there has been an encounter with a spiritual reality has added force.

The negative arguments for faith

Negative arguments by themselves can never be enough to show the truth of a philosophy of life, but they may form an important secondary support when a philosophy is challenged by what is claimed to be a more adequate alternative. I cannot possibly consider in this section all the alternatives that have been put forward, but I shall consider one of the most common, that of the secular humanist.

Unfortunately, the word 'humanism' is used to cover several different philosophies of life and, indeed, it referred in its origin to a movement within Christianity that stressed the importance of certain human values, especially some of those associated with the ancient classical world. Here, therefore, I shall only be concerned with one common variant which uses as its maxim the ancient saying 'Man is the measure of all things'[7] and which goes by the name of 'secular humanism'. Nor can what I say be applied directly to all humanists who use this slogan since they comprise such a variety of views.

There are two issues that I want to stress. The first relates to animals. If man is the measure of all things, then the only reason why animals should be respected and cared for is on account of their usefulness for man. For example, polar bears should be protected *because* we can enjoy looking at them, or hunting them, or *because* they are an important part of the ecology on which man himself depends. I do not deny that these are good reasons for protecting polar bears (except for hunting by those who do not really need their fur or meat), but I question whether this is an adequate account of why we should respect polar bears, or other animals. In a Christian view of nature, they are part of God's creation and we can give them an importance and dignity that need not be related to the human need of them. In my own view, we should even say that they have some sort of right to be there and to be protected in the enjoyment of their territory, except when there is some pressing human urgency, for example, when they endanger a human child, or when native people need them for their livelihood. Unfortunately, Christians have all too often failed to see this implication of the doctrine of creation and have tended to exploit the animal kingdom as much as any, in part through an unfortunate interpretation of Genesis.[8] However, at least the Christian philosophy allows for, and in my view demands, a positive philosophy of the animal kingdom, whereas a philosophy based on the maxim 'Man is the measure of all things' *cannot in principle*. But if a secular humanist abandons this maxim, then it is incumbent on him to state very clearly what he means by humanism.

The second issue goes even deeper, but is hard to bring out and I shall only indicate an issue which demands much thought. Most humanists wish to produce a philosophy of life in which man has a certain dignity and the high calling to realize a potential nobility. However, this can only be done by investing the notion of 'man' or of 'mankind' with some of the metaphysical attributes which Christians give to God. Thus, far from removing the difficulties that follow from introducing any discussion of 'higher purpose' or a 'spiritual reality', humanists tend to reintroduce the same difficulties, but without realizing that they do so. The metaphysical implications are hidden or disguised in all the talk of secularism and the denial of God. But what enduring significance or status can man have, if he is truly the measure of all things?

The witness of personal experience

When most Christians are asked by a friend, 'Why do you believe?', they are unlikely to give any of the arguments so far discussed, although when pressed they might well use some of them as supporting arguments. The most likely reply to the question is one which quotes personal experiences. As we have seen, these can take many forms; there may have been an experience of the numinous, or of loving support and a sense of inner strength, especially during a time of crisis, or there may have been an overwhelming sense of forgiveness and of a load of sin being taken away. Alternatively, there may have been outward events that have seemed either extraordinarily providential or miraculous, such a friend's recovery from a serious illness. Any of these experiences or events may lead a person to the belief that he has had an intimation of spiritual reality, as when the poet Francis Thompson says:

> I dimly guess what Time in mists confounds;
> Yet ever and anon a trumpet sounds
> From the hid battlements of Eternity;
> Those shaken mists a space unsettle, then
> Round the half-glimpsèd turrets slowly wash again.[9]

It is clearly impossible for an outsider to evaluate the inner experiences that seem to provide such intimations and, in most cases, almost impossible for him to evaluate the outside events that strike one person as providential or miraculous, for the force of such events often depends on the significance they have within the life of the Christian. In other words, we are not here concerned with general arguments, addressed to all men and women, but with inner experiences or outward events that can only have the force of an argument or of a witness to an individual.

Provided that the individual observes the warnings that I shall mention, I cannot see why experiences such as those described should not be taken seriously as possible indications of contact with a spiritual reality. Whereas in the Middle Ages it was important to warn people against superstition, it is as important now to warn people not only of superstitition in its twentieth-century dress, but equally of the irrational materialism which many people just assume to be a necessary part of scientific or rational thought. There is nothing in the nature of science, nor in the inquiring and critical rational faculty, to indicate that there is *not* a spiritual reality behind and beyond the reality that we find through our five senses. Atheism and materialism are just as much *interpretations* of our experience as is Christianity or some other spiritual view of the universe. Reason, in itself, should not start with a presumption either way, but as soon as it begins a critical reflection, then it seems to me that the indications that support a spiritual interpretation of the universe have the greater force.

If we seek an unblind faith, there are two warnings that should be heeded when we seek to base any faith on personal experience. First, we must be aware that there are several possible interpretations of any experience and, therefore, that we must not simply jump for the one that suits us or attracts us, without consideration of the alternatives. Second, what appears to be a private revelation of some kind must be tested to see if it is *contrary* to rational judgment or to our basic moral convictions,[10] remembering Jesus' warning 'You will know them by their fruits.'[11] The point here is that it is one thing for a personal revelation to show us something that *goes beyond* our present understanding and that demands that we enlarge our vision; it is quite another thing for an (apparent) revelation to *go against* the rational or the good. We have to assume that if the Christian God is a reality, he is a God of truth and of justice, and if we allow our experience to be interpreted in a way that does violence to truth or goodness, then we are heading for a blind faith and the possibility of the horrors of Jones-town!

Having noted these warnings that should be carefully observed by anyone who has personal experiences of a dramatic kind, we may then see these experiences as an important and legitimate part of the life of faith. Without them life would be duller, many of our insights would remain undiscovered and, above all, many people would lack that sense of personal warmth which fills out our understanding of God's love. For too many, the notion of God's love is confined to an intellectual idea. It should also become a living and warming experience and such it is in the daily life of many ordinary Christians.

XV Prayer and Work

Theory and practice

An adequate account of any religion ought to look at it from several viewpoints. In this book, I have been primarily concerned with what might be called the 'theoretical' aspect of Christianity, namely the fundamentals of what Christians believe. However, I want to acknowledge the equal importance of what might be called the 'practical' aspect of Christianity, that is its spiritual life, its rituals, its moral code and so on. This practical side of Christianity might also be described as the *activity* of the Christian faith, at church, at home, at work and at prayer.

Although the distinction that I have just made is real, it is important to see that it is impossible to draw a sharp line between the theory and the practice of Christianity, for what is truly believed is bound to affect what kinds of persons we are and how we act. Also, what we do is bound up with how we *understand* what we are doing. For example, if I have a sense of vocation, this is likely to affect both what activities I devote myself to and the manner in which I do them. The result of this is that a book on the fundamentals of Christian belief needs to say something on the more practical side of Christianity, especially in respect to the nature of prayer and of work, both of which raise certain problems for the thoughtful Christian.

Prayer and magic

In the next four sections, I am not concerned with practical instruction on how to pray, for which the reader must look elsewhere,[1] but with an understanding of what a prayer is and what it is not.

In the first place, prayer is not an attempt to change God's mind. This can be seen by stressing the important distinction between religion and magic that goes back to the work of Frazer[2] and other anthropologists who have studied both. Religion and magic are often found intermingled in our actual experience, including that of the Christian churches, but in principle they are very different. In magic, the aim is to control, or to manipulate for one's own purpose, God, or the gods or spiritual forces of an ill-defined sort. Magic is believed to work by a sort of lever principle that is almost mechanical, provided that one accepts the 'solidarity' between things that is part of the mentality of many primitive people. Rain, for example, is literally interconnected with the secret name for rain, or with the god of rain, or with a ritual dance that is symbolic of rain. Thus, by invoking the name of rain or of the rain-god, or by acting out a rain dance, one tends actually to produce rain because one has, as it were, operated the appropriate lever. Similarly, by invoking the name of God or of a god, especially a secret and 'real' name, then one somehow 'conjures' the deity and forces it to respond. More generally, any imagined use of spiritual force for one's own ends is suggestive of this ancient magical outlook and it is for this reason that it is easy to think of examples within the practice of many religious people.

By contrast, with religion in its pure form, instead of making spiritual forces work for us, we put ourselves at the service of God, or the gods. Indirectly, there may be some benefit for us, such as the joy of communion with God, but this i snot the purpose of true worship, as we have seen elsewhere. In a mature Christianity, we love because he first loved us[3] and consequently heaven may be the *result* of the good life, but it cannot be its *motive*, for otherwise we can have only a shallow copy of the good life.

The rejection of magical attitudes to religion should begin to make clear why true prayer is not the attempt to change God's mind. The conclusion is strengthened by the realization that there is something ludicrous in the very idea of God changing his mind, once we have grasped what the Christian idea of God is (with a certain reservation that I shall make in pp. 136–137). God already loves what he has made and no request of ours can make him love his creatures more, or give special preference to one as we might to a favourite child or friend. God has no favourites in this sense, although in another way we are all God's favourites. In a paradoxical way, no one is especially important and yet everyone is infinitely important!

Three stages of growth

The true meaning of prayer may be understood more fully if we take note of three stages in the spiritual life that many Christians pass through.

The first stage is proper and appropriate for the religion of a young child. Here God is highly personal and modelled on the kindest and worthiest adults that the child knows. As we have seen, some Christians never grow beyond this stage and the result is either a quite inadequate religion, or, more often, a rejection of God (but strictly speaking this is not a rejection of God himself, but of an inadequate picture of God).

The second stage develops through a reaction against the childish anthropomorphism of the first stage. The stress now is on the spiritual and moral laws that govern all things. Much or all of the talk about God is seen as symbolic and, in the anxiety to avoid false or infantile beliefs, the personal nature of God is played down, sometimes to vanishing point. Congruously, the emphasis on personal reward, or on an after-life with God, is put aside. (We have already noted the apparently surprising fact that surveys of opinion among church members show that many of them believe in no personal survival.) What matters is to live the life of love, following the example of Jesus as nearly as we are able.

The third stage, which I believe represents that of the mature Christian, involves a return to the idea that God is personal, but not in the simple-minded way that was appropriate to the first stage. The thing that allows for a return to the view that God is indeed personal, without relapsing into a childish faith, is the realization that what we mean by 'person', in relation to every person, needs to develop. The selfish ego, to which we all naturally wish to cling, is an inheritance from our animal nature. It is not in itself evil, but it is something which we have to learn to transcend, as we die to the old self, otherwise it can *become* a source of evil. Moreover, it is not as if we could have become true persons directly, without going through the stage of having an animal ego. This is something I tried to bring out in the discussion of evolution. Human 'personhood', like human goodness, is an *achievement* that has to be reached by a process of growth as we emerge from one level of living to another. Thus the childish ego and the childish faith in a personal God of stage one are not *wrong* for that stage. What is wrong is to stay at that stage. It is often a realization of this that leads to stage two, but this reaction is too negative. The Christian synthesis builds both on the simple faith of the child and on the insights of stage two and returns to belief in a personal God, but with a more mature idea of what 'personal' means. There is the dying of an old idea and an old ego, but the birth of something new. 'Unless a grain of wheat falls into the earth and dies, it remains alone . . .'

With the arrival of the third stage, the whole nature of petitionary prayer takes on a new appearance. There is something absurd in asking for personal favours, but nothing at all absurd in asking for what we need in order to fulfil our lives as Christians. As Augustine puts it, 'God does not ask us to tell him our needs in order that he may learn about them, but in order that we may be made capable of receiving his gifts.'[4] Hence the prayer 'Give us this day our daily bread' is absolutely appropriate once we realize the symbolic meaning of bread; and likewise the prayer for forgiveness and for strength. Also, since we are meant to retain some personal relationship with God, analogous to the relationship of child to parent, there is no reason why we should not ask God about other things that are in our hearts, whether in relation to ourselves or to other people, provided that: (1) we believe that these things are good (i.e. they are not just for our selfish satisfaction); and (2) we pray 'in his name', which means within the context of a relationship 'in Christ' in which we only expect to be granted what is for the good. It is in this context that Jesus promised that prayer would be answered[5] and we should note that this promise was made in the overall context of Jesus' saying 'I am the vine, you are the branches.'[6] The fact that prayer within this relationship does not rule out asking for specific things that are in our hearts is proved by Jesus' own prayer at the garden of Gethsemane: 'My Father, if it be possible, let this cup pass from me.' But we note that Jesus then continued, 'Nevertheless, not as I will, but as thou wilt.'[7]

Can prayer make a difference?

The question still remains, 'Can petitionary prayer actually make a difference?' We have seen that God's mind will not be changed by prayer, but at the same time we are told to pray for the sick and suffering. Is this kind of prayer only meant to change our attitudes? Or is it only meant to stir up the one who prays so that he or she will do something?

I believe that there is more to prayer than changing our attitude, or even stirring us to action, hence the reservation made in *Prayer and Magic*. The basis for this is our understanding of God's creation, which I have insisted to be an order, or an inter-related system, which has its own laws. One consequence of this emphasis is that, unless God is to resort to miracles at every moment, there are many things that God can only work through us, as a part of the created order. But this means more than God working through our hands, although this is indeed one way in which prayer may be answered. (As when a doctor prays for the suffering in a poor country and then feels moved to go and work there himself.) There is also the strange way in which we are inter-connected with the whole created order, and especially with our fellow man, at the spiritual level. Part of this interconnection may be indicated by telepathy, part by what Jung called the 'collective unconscious'.[8] Whatever the mechanisms involved, about which we may well be agnostic, it could be that my very concern for someone or something, and my mental reflection or my loving concern, may in itself slightly alter the balance of forces that are at work and which together cause change. Thus what God may wish to do, he may now be more able to do, just because this balance of spiritual forces is different.

If not pushed too far, the following analogy may be helpful for the situation that arises when one person prays for another, or even if he simply has a loving concern for him. We can think of God as a great radio transmitter and each person as a small receiver with a small transmitter attached to it. Let us suppose that for some reason A's receiver cannot hear God's transmission because of some fault, but that B, who is a friend of A, manages to act as a relay station, passing on God's message or God's power through his own small transmitter. A may be open to B in a way that he is not open to God.

On the basis of this analogy and making use of the principle that God not only chooses to work through people, but in many cases has set up an order that demands that he work through people, it is not hard to see how prayer might really make a difference on some occasions, without having to assume that God somehow changes his mind.

Prayer and petitionary prayer

In the previous sections, we have thought of prayer primarily in terms of petitionary prayer, that is of *asking* for something. However, in order to see the problem of the answer to prayer in proper perspective, we have to remember that petitionary prayer is only a small part of prayer, except perhaps at the first of the three stages. Prayer is equally a listening or waiting upon God, often in silence, sometimes with just a few words indicating adoration, thanksgiving, or penitence. If we ask, 'Does prayer make a difference?' when we are thinking of prayer in these forms, the question seems out of place. There may indeed be a difference made to ourselves, but this is not the purpose of such prayers. As we have seen earlier,[9] worship is to be understood in terms of a response and recognition of what is due to God, not in terms of what man can gain.

It does not follow that problems about the effect of petitionary prayer are unimportant, for even at the third stage petitionary prayer is a legitimate part of prayer, as we have seen from the practice of Jesus; but in the context of the wider meaning of prayer the problem looks very different. The chief emphasis in an understanding of prayer should be its role as an expression of our relationship with God and, through God, with our fellow man and the whole of God's creation.

Work and prayer

For the Christian who has come to see his whole life as a response to God's love, there cannot be a fundamental distinction between work and prayer. Our response includes thought, word and action and each of these affects, and is affected by, the others. There is a splendid passage in the book of Ecclesiasticus that reminds us of this. It describes the various occupations of man and their role in the life of a nation, with the strong implication that the intellectual should in no way look down on the person who works with his hands, for 'without these shall not a city be inhabited'. After stressing the fact that those who work with their hands will not understand things that concern the wise, the passage concludes, 'But they will maintain the fabric of the world; and in the handywork of their craft is their prayer.'[10]

It is a mistake to interpret this passage to mean that only in the case of artisans is work an extension of prayer. It applies equally to the occupation of anyone who realizes what work is really about. The root of this realization goes back to our philosophy of man, not only as a being who is struggling to emerge from the animal to the spiritual level, but also as a necessarily social being whose true self is bound up with his relationship to his fellow man. Our work is part of the way in which we contribute to the social order, or the way in which we 'tend' it, given our particular gifts and opportunities, just as Adam in the parable 'tended' the garden in which he was placed.

Unfortunately, man has created a world where it is impossible, or almost impossible, for some men and women to find work at all, or any work that has the dignity of helping to run the social order and contribute to the legitimate wants and needs of man. Since useful occupation is such an important element in our response to God and in achieving human dignity, it is vital that Christians concern themselves with this problem of unemployment. The implications of this for the spiritual richness or poverty of man are enormous. This is one of the reasons why I stressed the importance of Marx's thought at the end of chapter XIII.

Another question that is affected by a proper understanding of work is 'What kinds of work can a Christian properly undertake?' Part of the answer must be that any job that is important for the human social order, including occupations such as street cleaning, are legitimate and potentially dignified forms of work. A Christian may have the conviction that he has a particular talent that ought to be used in one of the more classical professions, but this is absolutely no grounds for any feeling of superiority.

However, there is an aspect of the question 'What kinds of work can a Christian properly undertake?' which is much harder to answer. Should a Christian accept a job that he sees as socially parasitic and useless, such as being a clerk in a gambling club, if this is the only kind of job that he can find in order to maintain his family? I can see no easy answer to this, but as the occupation gets further and further from social usefulness, then one would need increasingly strong grounds for accepting it, until with occupations that one considers intrinsically wrong, it is hard to see any possible grounds for taking them on. A similar problem arises when the acceptance of a job helps to maintain part of a social system that the Christian feels ought not to exist, or ought at least to be drastically reformed. In this case, a crucial question for the Christian to consider is this: 'If I accept this job will I simply be helping to maintain a system that I believe ought to be changed, or will I have some opportunity for working towards a change in the system from within?'

Two senses of 'vocation'

The discussion of the kinds of occupation that are suitable for the Christian leads naturally into the question of Christian vocation. Many people are confused about this because the word 'vocation' is used in two somewhat different senses within the context of the Christian faith. In one sense, which I call the primary sense, every Christian has a vocation. 'Vocation' literally means 'calling' and St Paul speaks of the calling of his readers when he says, 'Lead a life worthy of the calling to which you have been called.'[11] This is a reference to the way in which we are all called to respond to God's love and to show this response in the way in which we live. Within this primary sense of vocation, every Christian should be concerned with what work he does, for example by thinking about its social usefulness, and with the manner in which the work is done, for example, the energy and cheerfulness that are shown.

Christians also use the word 'vocation' in a secondary or derivative sense, although it may be the more familiar to some. This is when a Christian believes that he or she has a specific call to a particular task or profession, most traditionally as priest, doctor or teacher, but in principle to any worthwhile occupation. In such cases, Christians may not have worked out that this is the task or the role that their talents suggest, but they may well have had what seemed to be a 'call' in the form of a private religious experience. Sometimes it is as if a voice had actually spoken, sometimes it is more a growing conviction that is felt to come from God.

Naturally enough, when we are dealing with private religious experiences such as these, the same warnings apply as those discussed at the end of chapter XIV. If an apparent call conflicts with common sense, then we must suspect that we have misinterpreted our experience. However, there are limits to rational tests for a divine call, as the examples of Abraham and of Moses well illustrate.[12] There are also many recent examples of Christians who have responded to calls that seemed crazy to their friends, but who achieve a success which was thought to be impossible.

The challenge and excitement of a Christian life

When I was a small boy I used to wish that I lived in an age or place of real adventure. I wanted to have fought in the Wars of the Roses, or to have taken part in some of the adventures recounted by Tolkein. I think that I am now more realistic. One reason is that I have some idea what it would actually have been like to have fought in the Wars of the Roses, which for those taking part were anything but romantic. However, the most substantial reason is that every human life has all the drama and excitement it needs, if only we can be sensitive to the significance of what is going on within us and around us. Let me try to describe this in terms of three concentric circles.

First, and most immediately, there is the battle within the inner circle of our own selves. Becoming a person is a process of emergence which involves a spiritual struggle that is every bit as dramatic and significant as the battles we can read about in history. Moreover, this is the one battle in which *we* are always able to play a decisive role. If the Christian faith is true, then, with the help of God, here is a battle that we *can* win, but which we may easily not win. Sometimes the battle seems like a boring grind, but it can hardly be more of a boring grind than the actual campaigns, which we tend to romanticize, really were. The proper way to see these periods of tedium is as challenges of a special sort, for the painful side of the struggle against evil within us is only sometimes manifested in an obvious crisis of conscience, as when we face a dramatic temptation. Equally important is the challenge to accept the periods of growth in which nothing seems to be happening and when boredom itself is part of the temptation.

Second, there is the circle of our friends and others with whom we are in immediate contact. Although each person has his or her private story, we can profoundly influence other people through the way in which we represent the good, or fail to represent it. My friend or neighbour's fall or despair is, in part, my fault, for we are our brother's keeper. If I take a bribe, or get involved in a shady business deal, or fail to do my best to make my marriage a success, or fail in one of the countless other situations that I face, I contribute to the decay of society and the injustices of the world. It is amazing how many outwardly respectable people are involved in one kind of misdeed or another, or are failing to fulfil some basic duty towards others and, because the effects on other people are not always obvious, such actions or lack of actions tend to be condoned by the conscience. 'Anyway, everybody's doing it,' we tend to say. But in what we do and in what we do not do, we help to create the quality of life around us. If people matter, can one ask for something more significant than this?

Third, there is the level of the world order, about which we so often feel helpless. What can I do about the torture of political prisoners, or starving children, or the pollution of the atmosphere and so on? But of course, it is precisely because most people take this attitude that they can do nothing about such things that these problems exist. We can make a small difference, through the way we wage our personal battle and the battle at the level of the second circle; it is only by everyone taking these battles seriously that the global battle can be fought. Moreover, in some cases we can have a direct input, albeit a very small one, in the global battle, for example, by supporting an organization that works for political prisoners, or starving children, or by working for them.

All told, there is no lack of exciting and meaningful adventure in this world; the problem is our blindness to the significance of what is right in front of us.

Finally, let me attempt to link the foregoing remarks to the theme of love and that first commandment without which everything else is wasted. Love is the theme that binds together the theoretical understanding of the Christian faith, with which I have been primarily concerned throughout this book, and the practical side of the Christian faith.

Let us suppose that we are looking back over our lives a few hours before death, say from a known disease or from execution. What is it that we shall most regret? Surely, with the sense of perspective that this situation will give us, many of the things that we have cherished will seem futile. What does it really matter that I landed that job, or had that reputation, or made that money? Soon I shall be dead and then all these things will mean nothing. But there are some things that we shall look back on with a sense of real satisfaction. 'Well, whatever happens, that was good!' If we have any sense of real values, these things will involve the awareness of something beautiful, especially in the form of some good relationship with other people. 'That was a real friendship; Mary and I really had something going together; that was a great time when we were all together as a family; and so on.' Similarly, the things that we shall most regret will be failures in matters that concern those close to us. 'If only . . .' Perhaps the greatest pains of the next life, for the good and for the bad, will be the sense of having missed this and that opportunity to love someone, an opportunity that can never be repeated. Think of the potential pain of the truly evil man if ever he grows enough to realize the vastness of the opportunities for love that he has missed. Perhaps this is the real meaning of hell.

But the last note must be of hope. The Christian believes that love is not only the highest value, in terms of which his life must be measured, it is also the name for that ultimate reality that has set up this whole order and governs it in his own mysterious way, using earthen vessels like ourselves. So although what has not been done in the name of love represents a tragic loss, there is the future and the prospect of creative action to come, both in the rest of this life and for all eternity.

Notes

Chapter I Faith and Reason

1. E.g. Matt. 5.8; Luke 9.62.
2. I Peter 3.15. Bible translations are from the Revised Standard Version, except where otherwise indicated.
3. Isa. 6.5; Job 42.3–6.
4. I Cor. 13.12.
5. See the essay by William James, *The Will to Believe*, 1897 (and many later editions).
6. See Acts 19.5; I Cor. 12.3 and chapter IX, *Level A. Christ is Lord*.
7. I Cor. 15.3–8.
8. E.g. Leslie D. Weatherhead, *The Christian Agnostic*, Hodder & Stoughton and Abingdon 1965.
9. John 1.14.
10. Jer. 29.13 (translation from the oratorio).

Chapter II The Idea of God

1. Josh. 6.21; 8.1–2, 24–8.
2. I Kings 20.
3. Ps. 33.12.
4. II Sam. 6.6–7.
5. Micah 6.8.
6. Isa. 5.16.
7. Anaxagoras, born about 500 BC.
8. Gen. 1.27.
9. See R. Otto, *The Idea of the Holy*, Oxford University Press 1923.
10. Ex. 3.14.
11. Mark 14.36; cf. Rom. 8.15 and Gal. 4.6.

Chapter III The Story of Man

1. Ps. 8.4.
2. Gen. 3.5.
3. The New Testament has several references to Jesus' brothers and sisters and many Christians have thought that these were children of Mary and

Joseph, born after Jesus, e.g. Mark 6.3; Gal. 1.19. The Roman Catholic view is that these were half-brothers and sisters of Jesus, born to Joseph by his first wife, and the Greek does not rule out this interpretation. However, the chief reason for the Roman Catholic view (which seems to go against the natural reading and the implication of Matt. 1.25) is the concern to exalt Mary. I agree with those who think that if Mary had children naturally, after the birth of Jesus, this in no way diminishes her stature. Hence, while I respect the doctrine of the virgin birth as both ancient and biblical, I am very doubtful of the alleged 'ever-virginity' of Mary. I much prefer to see her as a model for Christian marriage.

4. *Humani generis*, 12 August 1950.
5. The only way in which it could be meaningful to speak of individual guilt in a baby is if we accept reincarnation. Doctrines of collective guilt run into grave moral objections. See, for example, H. D. Lewis, *Morals and Revelation*, Allen & Unwin 1951, ch. 5.
6. 'Puritan' views of sex vary considerably, but I have in mind the view that sexual passion, even between married partners, should not be *enjoyed*. This view can still be found in both Roman Catholic and Protestant circles.
7. Jer. 31.29–30; cf. Ex. 20.5.
8. Gal. 5.17.
9. John 1.14; cf. II Cor. 5.16.

Chapter IV   Jesus is Lord

1. For example, in the hymn 'In the Bleak Mid-Winter', verse 2.
2. John 1.1.
3. Col. 1.15; cf. Heb. 1.3.
4. Matt. 16.16.
5. Mark 2.5–7.
6. Matt. 5.38–9; cf. Ex. 21.24.
7. Matt. 11.4.
8. John 10.38; cf. Matt. 8.4. On many occasions Jesus asked those whom he had healed not to spread the miracle abroad.
9. John 8.58.
10. E.g. I Kings 22.17.
11. Mark 13.2; cf. Matt. 23.37–8.
12. Isa. 42.6.
13. II Cor. 5.19.
14. John 1.14.
15. *De incarnatione verbi*, 54 PG25, 192B; cf. Gal. 4.4–7.
16. E.g. Acts 2.38; 10.48.

Chapter V   Jesus is Saviour

1. Heb. 4.15.
2. Matt. 26.53.

3. cf. Phil. 2.5–8.
4. *Nicomachean Ethics* 3.5, 1113b–1115a. In Aristotle genuine virtue is an *acquired* disposition.
5. Ibid., 6.13, 1144b.
6. I Cor. 15.22 (RV).
7. I John 4.19.
8. John 12.32.
9. See the hymn 'My God, I love thee; not because I hope for heaven thereby, . . .' Also ch. VIII, reference 2.
10. *Republic* 361, 364; cf. *Apology* 28a.
11. Mark 2.17.
12. P. Tillich, *The Courage To Be*, Yale University Press, Nisbet 1952 and Fontana ed. 1962, ch. 6.
13. John 12.24–5.
14. John 14.20; 15.5.
15. Rom. 6.3–5.
16. John Donne, 'The Bell', *Devotions upon emergent occasions, Complete Poetry and Selected Prose*, ed. John Hayward, Nonesuch Press 1929, p. 538.

Chapter VI Father, Son and Holy Spirit

1. Isa. 63.16; Ps. 89.26.
2. Ps. 104.24 (Prayer Book translation).
3. Isa. 6.3.
4. Heb. 1.2–3.
5. John 3.8.
6. Acts 2.1–4.
7. E.g. Judg. 14.19.
8. Rom. 8.26–7.
9. *De Trinitate* VIII, ch. 10 (VIII, 14).
10. Ibid., books IX and X.
11. Ibid., XV, ch. 17 (XV, 31) (S. McKenna's translation).
12. D. Sayers, *The Mind of the Maker*, Methuen 1941.
13. Hegel's Trinity is that of Idea, Nature and Spirit and he saw his elaboration of this Trinity as an exposition of Christian doctrine.
14. E.g. Prov. 8.22–end, especially v.30.
15. E.g. Acts 19.5–6.
16. W. James, *The Varieties of Religious Experience*, Longmans Green & Co 1902, Fontana 1960, lectures 4 and 5.
17. Provided that we are speaking of 'natural numbers' or 'positive integers', i.e. 1,2,3, . . .; cf. Descartes' fourth meditation for a similar view of human freedom.
18. Because of its familiarity, we tend to take our awareness and our self-awareness for granted. However, every now and then we can be struck with sheer amazement at the fact of these gifts. We are not 'things', but

centres of feeling and thought. This can give us a glimpse of God's awareness of all that he has made.

19. Although human love is grounded in animal affection, it can develop into something infinitely richer. In the true love of a friend, or in the feeling of universal compassion, we have another glimpse into the mind of God.

20. Christian philosophy has long insisted that God is 'Being' or 'Existence', partly because of the name of God revealed to Moses (Ex. 3.14) and partly because God is the source of all that is. However, man's being or existence is *dependent* on God's, whereas God's Being or Existence must be dependent on nothing outside itself. Therefore, man's 'being' is analogous to God's 'Being' in a different sense (of analogy) than his freedom is analogous to God's freedom.

Chapter VII Church and Sacrament

1. E.g. II Cor. 1.7; Phil. 3.10; I Peter 4.13.
2. I Cor. 12.12–4.
3. Matt. 16.18.
4. Matt. 7.16.
5. II Cor. 4.7.
6. Prayer Book catechism.
7. In John, the last supper appears to have taken place the night before the passover; in the other gospels, on the passover night itself.
8. I Cor. 11.23–6.
9. John 6.63.

Chapter VIII Life and Eternal Life

1. J. Locke, *The Reasonableness of Christianity* (1695), *Works*, VII, pp. 150–1 in the 1823 edition.
2. No. 80 in *The English Hymnal*.
3. cf. Gen. 2.7. In general the Old Testament word *nephesh*, which is usually translated as 'soul', is used in this way and not for an entity that could exist without a body.
4. Mark 12.24–7.
5. I Cor. 15.14.
6. H. Wambach, *Reliving Past Lives: The Evidence Under Hypnosis*, Harper & Row 1978 and Hutchinson 1979.
7. I. Stevenson, *Cases of the Reincarnation Type*, University Press of Virginia 1975.
8. 'Paranormal' refers to faculties, or alleged faculties, such as telepathy and clairvoyance. A paranormal explanation would be contrasted with a scientific or 'naturalistic' explanation.
9. See, for example, E. L. Ladurie, *Montaillou*, Penguin 1980, pp. 163, 194, 206, 209, 291–2, 325, 352.
10. See ch. III, section 5.
11. John 14.2.

12. Mark 15.34.
13. Matt. 25.13.
14. Matt. 25.44–5.

Chapter IX The Essentials and the Non-essentials

1. See ch. I, *Unblind faith*.
2. Acts 2.38.
3. It must be stressed that the basic Christian commitment includes *both* the attempt to follow the moral teachings of Jesus *and* his way of prayer. From ch. I, it should be clear that prayer of a kind is possible even during periods of doubt.
4. J. S. Mill, *On Liberty*, Oxford University Press 1975, especially ch. 2.
5. The grounds include respect for an ancient tradition and the practical benefits of having a 'pastor of the pastors'. (There are also, it must be admitted, some negative practical aspects!) If the claim that Christ himself instituted the episcopal ministry could be established, this would, of course, virtually settle the argument. Unfortunately, the historical evidence for this claim is ambiguous.

Chapter X Evil and Suffering

1. E.g. Ps. 73.3–5.
2. Ps. 37.36–7 (Prayer Book translation).
3. In translations of the Old Testament, we often find the word 'almighty' for the Hebrew *shaddai*. The Hebrew suggests one who is mighty, but not necessarily one who can do literally *anything*.
4. E.g. Matt. 19.26.
5. Michael J. Langford, *Providence*, SCM Press 1981.

Chapter XI The Problem of Freedom

1. Gal. 4.8–11.
2. There are some philosophers who think that man can be both scientifically determined and 'free' in a significant sense. I believe that this view is mistaken, but I have not the space to explore it here.
3. However, strictly scientific arguments or discoveries can have some relevance to the issue. For example, further discoveries about the nature of the brain might make the determinist position more or less plausible.
4. See E. R. Dodds, *The Greeks and the Irrational*, University of California Press 1951, ch. 8. Also J. P. Sartre's play, *Huis Clos*.
5. I Cor. 15.10.
6. Rom. 5.8.
7. There is a more general sense of 'grace' that refers to the gifts of God that we need continually, even to exist. In this sense, of course, no achievement is possible without grace.

Chapter XII The Bible: History, Myth, or Legend?

1. I do not think that Christianity would disappear completely, but it would lose many followers and those who remained would have to reinterpret many of the basic doctrines. It would probably become very similar to Mahayana Buddhism.
2. C. H. Dodd, *The Founder of Christianity*, Fontana 1973, p. 27.
3. Judg. 1.8.
4. Judg. 1.21; Josh. 15.63.
5. Some fundamentalists try to avoid this objection by claiming that if God commands the slaughter of women and children, or anything else, this makes it right. However, this is a desperate line of defence, for it renders the statement 'God is good' totally meaningless, for 'good' is defined purely in terms of God's will. Traditional Christianity has always rejected this view of morality, claiming that goodness is rooted in God's whole nature, not just his will.
6. If Revelation were proved to be a late first century book, which it might possibly be, this would not alter the main point. The value of a book in the Bible is not the result of it being dictated by God, but the result of the context in which it was written and the insights of the author. The gospels, and most of Paul's letters, are *primary* texts, while Revelation is *secondary*. In general, the apocrypha is a collection of secondary material that has less significance than primary material which contains eye-witness accounts of the central events of the New Testament.
7. Matt. 13.22. It is important to note that only *some* of Jesus' parables are allegories. Some make just one point and then allegorization turns them into nonsense. An example of this is the parable of the unjust judge, Luke 18.1–8.
8. I Cor. 10.1–11; cf. Gal. 4.24.
9. Matt. 5.3–12; Luke 6.20–6.
10. E.g. Mark 10.35–41; cf. Matt. 20.20 and Mark 9.18; cf. Matt. 10.1 and Luke 10.17.
11. It is unlikely that anyone who proclaimed 'Jesus is Lord' would be unable to accept *any* of the three views of the resurrection that I have described. However, it is possible, hence the word 'almost' at this point.
12. By 'private' I do not necessarily mean 'individual', rather I mean that the encounters, whether to an individual or a group, could not be tested by scientific procedures open to all. Jesus' resurrection appearances were always to the faithful, with the possible exception of Paul.
13. Matt. 16.15.
14. For a further account of the nature of the Bible and of its authority, see my *Providence*, pp. 140–2.

Chapter XIII Christianity and Other Religions

1. Sometimes there is a fine line between 'a religion' and 'a great religion'. However, we do not need to study all primitive forms of religion in

depth in order to know that they contain large quantities of superstition. At the same time, it must be stressed that many primitive religions contain great insights and have a prime importance for the social life of a people.

2. Some Christians speculate that if there is intelligent life elsewhere in the universe, there may be equivalent incarnations there. Also, there is nothing impossible in the notion of Jesus' return to this earth, but if the purpose of the incarnation were a divine identification with mankind, then there is a strong case for claiming that this need happen only once (apart from the question of a second coming at the end of the age).

3. *Enchiridion* 16.

4. Rom. 12.15.

5. Mark 12.30.

6. Hinduism is divided into many schools and the particular contrast that I am making could not be applied to every school.

7. See chapter V, *Life 'in Christ'*.

8. See chapter X, *How far is freedom the answer?*, *Natural evil*.

9. See, for example, F. Engels, 'Ludwig Feuerbach' (1888), and V. I. Lenin, 'What the "Friends of the People" Are' (1894), quoted in *Reader in Marxist Philosophy*, ed. H. Selsam and H. Martel, International Publishers, New York 1963, pp. 193, 198. N.B. 'Now – since the appearance of *Capital* – the materialist conception of history is no longer a hypothesis, but a scientifically demonstrated proposition' (Lenin).

Chapter XIV The Rational Defence of the Christian Faith

1. See chapter I, *A purely rational faith?*

2. See C. A. Coulson, *Science and Christian Belief*, Oxford University Press, 1955, p. 22.

3. See chapter XII, note 5 and my *Providence*, p. 178, note 27.

4. For an interesting illustration of this point, see R. W. Hepburn, *Christianity and Paradox*, Pegasus 1968, pp. 44–6, 206.

5. E.g. *Totem and Taboo* (1913), *The Future of an Illusion* (1927), and *Moses and Monotheism* (1939).

6. I will give just two illustrations of this inadequacy. First, his view that religious faith is basically wish-fulfilment neglects the many examples of faiths that have believed in no personal after-life, but which have made exacting demands. Also, when personal survival is believed in, Freud does not appreciate the difference between survival as a *result* of, and as a *motive* for, faith. Second, his explanation of Jewish monotheism depends on an anthropological 'horde-theory' which is now generally discredited.

7. Protagoras, born about 490 BC.

8. See Gen. 1.28–30; 2.19–20. I suggest that the proper interpretation of these passages indicates man's responsibility, not his right of exploitation. I do not mean that the author of the passages necessarily realized

this, but that a Christian philosophy, founded in the New Testament, demands such an interpretation.

9. From 'The Hound of Heaven'.
10. Though sometimes we may be called upon to reconsider some of our moral convictions. However, we must be careful that we are not swayed by an overpowering emotion to go against a rational judgment.
11. Matt. 7.16.

Chapter XV Prayer and Work

1. For practical guidance on prayer, see Mark Gibbard, *Why Pray?*, SCM Press 1970, and other books by this author.
2. J. G. Frazer, *The Golden Bough*, Vol. 1 of the 12 vol. ed. of 1907–15, pp. 220 ff.; cf. B. Malinowski, *Magic, Science and Religion*, Anchor 1954, pp. 87ff.
3. I John 4.19.
4. *Ep.* 130 (To Proba), VIII, 17; PL33.500, quoted in P. R. Baelz, *Prayer and Providence*, SCM Press 1968, p. 112.
5. John 15.7, 16.
6. John 15.5.
7. Matt. 26.39.
8. See also Rom. 8.22.
9. See chapter II, *Faith and the idea of God*.
10. Ecclus. (Ben Sira) 38.24–34 (RV).
11. Eph. 4.1.
12. Gen. 12.1–4; Ex. 3.10–11.